NUEVO TEX MEX

FESTIVE NEW RECIPES FROM JUST NORTH OF THE BORDER

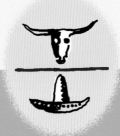

DAVid GARRIDO aNd RObb WALSH

FOReWOrd by STEphAN PyLes ★ PhoToGraphs by MaNNy RodRigueZ

CHRONICLE BOOKS

SAN FRANCISCO

Library of Congress Cataloging-in-Publication Data:

Garrido, David.
Nuevo Tex-Mex: festive new recipes from just north of the border
by David Garrido and Robb Walsh; foreword by Stephan Pyles;
photographs by Manny Rodriguez. p. cm.
Includes bibliographical references and index.
ISBN 0-8118-1612-5
1. Mexican American cookery. 2. Cookery, American—Southwestern
style. I. Walsh, Robb. II. Title.
TX715.2.S69G37 1998
641.59'268720764—dc21   97-30796 CIP

Coca-Cola® is a registered trademark of the Coca-Cola Company.
Fritos® is a registered trademark of Frito-Lay.

PRINTED IN HONG KONG.

Designed by Sibley/Peteet Design
Food Stylist: Brooke Leonard
Prop Stylist: Molly Terry
Assistant to Food Stylist: Martha Gooding
Assistants to Photographer: Timothy J. Garrison
and Adam A. Rodriguez
Food Stylist/Cover: Cheryl W. Binnie

Distributed in Canada by Raincoast Books
8680 Cambie Street
Vancouver, British Columbia V6P 6M9

10 9 8 7 6 5 4 3

CHRONICLE BOOKS
85 Second Street
San Francisco, California 94105

www.chroniclebooks.com

Table of Contents

ACKNOWLEDGMENTS

Stephan Pyles taught us to trust our instincts.
Bruce Auden taught us that to really taste food, you
have to close your eyes and hear what it says to
your soul. The authors wish to thank these two
visionaries of Texan cooking for all the inspiration
they have given us over the years.
We also wish to thank our agent, Patricia Van der Leun,
and Bill LeBlond of Chronicle Books for
making this project happen. Thanks to Rebecca
Rather and Marion Winik for their love and
support. And a special acknowledgment to Ron
Weiss, Alma Thomas, George Reiff,
and everybody at Jeffrey's for all the
assistance with this book.

*Dedicated to Alex and Danny Garrido and
Katie and Julia Walsh*

When I grew up in West Texas, Tex-Mex was everyday fare. At my parents' truck stop, chicken enchiladas and green chile pork tamales were on the menu along with the barbecue and chicken-fried steak. And at home there was always a bowl of jalapeños on the table.

A few purists dismiss Tex-Mex as a bastardization of authentic Mexican cooking, but it is actually a cuisine unto itself. To understand its history you have to keep in mind that Texas was a part of Mexico for nearly as long as it has been a part of the United States. Texas and Mexico may have been politically separated, but gastronomically they remain joined.

Over the years, processed cheese food and other shortcuts have found their way into many Tex-Mex *cocinas* and compromised the integrity of the cuisine. But in every Texas city, there are still Tex-Mex restaurants that have remained true to their time-honored cooking traditions—traditions rooted firmly in the peasant culture of Texas.

But for decades, Tex-Mex has grown in popularity both inside and outside the borders of Texas and as far away as Paris with very little stylistic change. Until now.

All cuisines need to be updated from time to time, and Nuevo Tex-Mex is a style whose time has come. With culinary artistry and a lively sense of humor, David Garrido and Robb Walsh have transformed the basic elements of Tex-Mex into a cuisine that is both comfortably familiar and entertainingly creative. Nuevo Tex-Mex takes the homey soul food of Texas to a new level of sophistication.

David is a Mexican national and a Texas chef. As a practitioner of Southwestern cuisine with a heritage deeply rooted in Mexico, David has a natural advantage. The Southwestern cuisine has always relied heavily on Mexican ingredients and Mexican techniques, and David has an affinity for the cooking of his native country that those of us who were born in the United States will never equal.

Of all the talented chefs who have ever worked for me and run my kitchen, no one has ever shown a greater depth of passion and knowledge than David. He has inspired more than one signature dish at Star Canyon and before that at Routh Street Cafe. David possesses a quality that allows the quantum leap from good chef to great chef and cannot be taught—intuition. An intuitive chef composes menus like symphonies, so that the individual ingredients come together in harmonious blends and vibrant explosions of flavors. David is just such a chef.

I first met Robb Walsh when he was the food editor of the Austin Chronicle and he called to ask me to come down and judge the Austin Hot Sauce Contest. Seven years and 732 hot sauces later, I still make the pilgrimage to Austin every year for a little palate-scorching fun with Robb and his band of chile heads. Fittingly enough, when Robb took his place among the top food writers in the country, winning the prestigious James Beard Journalism Award in 1996, it was for a magazine article titled "Hot Sauce Safari."

In his newspaper and magazine stories, and in his column in *Natural History Magazine*, Robb brings the culinary history and epicurean delights of the southwestern United States and Latin America to a national audience.

Now let this brilliant writer and chef introduce you to the hearty pleasures of a regional cuisine in tune with the twenty-first century—Nuevo Tex-Mex.

– Stephan Pyles

CLOSE YOUR EYES AND REMEMBER THE FIRST TIME YOU EVER DIPPED A CHIP IN GUACAMOLE. SAVOR THE RUSH OF GARLIC, THE SIMULTANEOUS bite of the jalapeño, and the squish of cool, creamy avocado on your tongue, then reach for the Corona with the lime pushed down inside. ✶ Now recall the thunderous crunch and the shower of lettuce that announced your first bite of a crispy taco. And the sentimental ending of the combination plate, when you first used a warm tortilla to mop up the delicious mess of chili sauce and cheese that the enchilada left behind.

Once upon a time, Americans fell in love with Tex-Mex, and the effects of this wave of infatuation are still rippling through modern American cuisine. Thanks to Tex-Mex, salsa has replaced ketchup as America's favorite condiment. Tacos and tortilla chips have reached a level of popularity rivaling the almighty hamburger and french fries. Chile peppers have become a national obsession, and the popularity of guacamole has moved the avocado from total obscurity to the front row of the produce section.

For some, the old love affair has lost its thrill, and there are even those who are ready to dump Tex-Mex into the bus tray of history. Food critics ridicule its Velveeta-veiled señorita platters, Mexican-cooking authorities question its legitimacy, and the watchdogs of the public health rail against its unsaturated fats.

Authentic Mexican food and Southwestern cuisine have become the upscale versions of border cuisine, while many equate Tex-Mex with junk food — greasy tacos, congealed mixed plates, and salsas that come in little plastic pillows.

But Tex-Mex has triumphed despite its criticisms. Authentic Mexican food and Southwestern cuisine have many fans, but in terms of popularity, they are no match for Tex-Mex. Despite its low-brow reputation at home, Tex-Mex has conquered the world. The wonders of crispy tacos are now being appreciated from Tokyo to Oman. Tex-Mex is the toast of France, where the locals are making cheese enchiladas with aged Gruyère on the Left Bank and debating new margarita recipes in the Dordogne.

As Tex-Mex spans the globe, it keeps evolving. Here at home, it's changing too. The old-fashioned señorita platter may have gone out of style, but something more exciting is taking its place. This cookbook is an introduction to the modern version of Texas Mexican cooking, a style we call Nuevo Tex-Mex.

Nuevo Tex-Mex brings our appreciation for authentic Mexican dishes and Southwestern cuisine back home to its Tex-Mex roots. It is spicy, eat-it-with-your-fingers food that combines modern ingredients with traditional, forthright flavors.

Tex-Mex is one of America's oldest regional cooking styles. The restaurants that started serving it at the turn of the last century, like the Original Mexican Restaurant in San Antonio and the Old Borunda Cafe in Marfa, are gone now. Nuevo Tex-Mex proves that their spirit lives on.

Here's to the next hundred years!

Tex-Mex: 1. Designating the Texan variety of something Mexican.

OXFORD ENGLISH DICTIONARY

The most famous Tex-Mex establishments have always called themselves Mexican restaurants, which is understandable, since when most of them first opened, Tex-Mex didn't exist.

When *Tex-Mex* first appeared in print in the 1940s, it referred to the half English–half Spanish lingo used along the border, the patois we now call Spanglish. It wasn't until the early 1970s that Tex-Mex gained its current association with food.

In her enormously respected cookbook *The Cuisines of Mexico*, published in 1972, Diana Kennedy drew the line between authentic interior Mexican food and the "mixed plates" we ate at "so-called Mexican restaurants" in the United States. Thereafter, food-savvy Americans (*savvy* is a Tex-Mex word, by the way, from the Spanish *saber*, "to know") began to make a distinction between authentic Mexican food and Tex-Mex.

According to the Oxford English Dictionary, the first use of Tex-Mex as a food term appeared in the following 1973 quote from the *News*, a Mexico City newspaper: "It is a mistake to come to Mexico and not try the local cuisine, it is not the Tex-Mex cooking one is used to in the United States."

The term *Tex-Mex* may have originally been intended as an insult, but the rest of the world found it catchy. For Europeans, the term evoked images of cowboys and indians and legends of the Wild West. The sophisticated, but somewhat baroque, cuisine of interior Mexico never really caught on internationally, but the crispy tacos, nachos, and margaritas of Tex-Mex soon became famous everywhere.

As its popularity spread, the negative connotations have subsided. The term is now used to describe a regional cuisine that combines Mexican and Texas cooking styles. Today, more and more "Mexican restaurants" in Texas are proud to call their food "Tex-Mex."

CHAPTER 1

¡Salud!

BEVERAGEs

PUT AWAY YOUR CHARDONNAY AND SAVE YOUR SAUVIGNON. LET'S DISCUSS THE NUANCES OF FLAVOR IN AN ICY COLD BEER. TEX-MEX IS *cerveza* cuisine. And, lucky for Nuevo Tex-Mex, a brewing renaissance is upon us. American microbrewers have not only reminded us how good beer can taste, they've also made ordering a cold one respectable again. ✹ Yes, that's right, we said "a cold one." We know some experts say that beer should be served lukewarm to be fully appreciated, but those experts don't live in Texas. ⚜ You know that style of rearview mirror that's glued to the middle of a car's windshield? Well, a couple of summers ago it got so hot here that people's rearview mirrors started melting off. Lukewarm beer is fine in a cold, damp pub in England, but in the hellishly hot environs of the borderland, keeping your beer cold is a science, an art form, and a tradition. We still call convenience stores ice houses in Texas because that's where we kept the beer before we had refrigerators.

So how do you go about choosing a beer to go with a particular Nuevo Tex-Mex dish? Well, don't bother reading the beer books. For some reason, several of the top beer writers in the world have the strange idea that the best thing to drink with a plate of spicy, chile pepper–flavored food is a spicy, chile pepper–flavored beer.

Drinking chile pepper beer with hot and spicy food makes about as much sense as trying to put out a fire with gasoline. When you're eating spicy food, you need a beverage to cool off your mouth. Almost any beer will do the trick — except chile pepper beer.

Of course, some beers go better with one thing than another. Malty porter and citrusy ceviche is a bit of a mismatch for instance. And crisp pilsner isn't our favorite brew for beef and mushrooms. So we've drawn up this handy chart. We've picked a few of our favorite styles and we've shown how we match them with foods. Make your own substitutions. (And if all this is too complicated, you have our permission to just drink whatever's in the fridge.)

Pilsners, Pale Ales, and India Pale Ales	Lime- or vinegar-flavored dishes like ceviche, salsas, salads
Light Lagers and Wheat Beers	Shrimp, seafood, chicken, tomato sauces
Blonde Ales, Medium Lagers, and Dry Stouts	Pork, fajitas, shark tacos
Bocks and Dark Lagers	Beef dishes, wild mushrooms, grilled onions
Brown Ales and Oatmeal Stouts	Duck, dark moles, black beans

The other beverage that has become part and parcel of the Tex-Mex experience is tequila. Over the years, tequila has acquired a somewhat mythic reputation. At the risk of ruining a good yarn, we have to report that regardless of your hallucinatory inebriations, tequila and mezcal are not made from the cactus that produces mescaline. And no, tequila is not distilled from pulque. And while we're at it, it's mezcal de Oaxaca that has the worms in it, not tequila.

Like cognac and champagne, tequila is a liquor that's named for a place. The name of the liquor is properly *mezcal de Tequila*. Mezcal, a distilled spirit made from the fermented hearts of a large succulent called maguey, is produced in many parts of Mexico. But *mezcal de Tequila* is by far the most famous. In 1873, the town of Tequila, Jalisco, was already shipping its famous mezcal to Texas and New Mexico. In 1893, a mezcal from Tequila took a prize at the Chicago World's Fair. By the turn of the century, the town and the liquor had become synonymous. Nowadays, the tequila-producing region has been expanded to include parts of several states around the old town.

The distinctive flavor of tequila comes from the blue agave variety of maguey. Other varieties of maguey are used to make mezcal and pulque in other parts of Mexico. Pulque is a thick, foamy beverage with an alcohol content similar to beer and a history that goes back to pre-Columbian times. Mezcal was invented by the Spaniards, who were thirsty for something with a little more punch.

Tequila is rated according to age. The *plata*, or silver variety, is colorless and is bottled immediately after distilling. Gold tequilas are tinted with caramel coloring. *Reposados*, or "rested tequilas," are aged for a short time in wood casks. Añejo tequilas are aged for up to seven years in wood and sometimes have a cognaclike smoothness; they are by far the most expensive.

In the mid-1980s, tequila began to become fashionable, and some very good brands like Herradura and Chinaco have since attained cult status in the international market. The Japanese, in particular, have bought up huge amounts and driven up the prices of these labels. In response, some producers have begun to produce estate-bottled, 100-percent blue agave tequilas that they sell in elaborately designed bottles. Some of these super-premium tequilas sell for forty dollars a bottle and more.

A few years ago, we got together a dozen veteran tequila drinkers and conducted a blind tasting to see how much all this really mattered. We included some super-premium tequilas, some famous old brand names, and a couple of ringers to see if anybody could really tell the difference. Here's what we found:

The Rankings

Our panel of eight judges included bartenders, journalists, and tequila addicts. Here is the way they rated the eight tequilas.

Tequila	Score (out of 20)	Price (for 750 ml)
Herradura Añejo	18.1	$40
El Tesoro Muy Añejo	17.7	$35
Torada (Reposado)	17.1	$8
Cuervo (Gold)	16.6	$16
El Tesoro Plata	16.5	$30
Dos Reales Plata	15.1	$27
Sauza Tres Generationes	13.1	$30
Sauza Hornitos	12.8	$17

The biggest shocker here is Torada, a bargain brand with a terribly gaudy label. While we were shopping for our taste-test tequilas, we told our favorite liquor store owner what we were up to, and he suggested that Torada be one of our ringers. It looked suspicious, but he let us in on a little secret. Torada is actually a well-made Mexican tequila that is shipped across the border in tanker cars. It is bottled in New Orleans, which saves a lot of money on duty and shipping. Available in *plata* or *reposado*, Torada sells for a fraction of what premium tequilas cost. The liquor store owner bet that our tasters wouldn't be able to tell the difference. He was right.

There are also bargain brands of tequila on store shelves that aren't very good, so you can't assume that any gaudy label will do. But if you're making margaritas, you can save yourself a few bucks by asking a knowledgeable store owner to recommend an inexpensive, high-quality tequila that is made in Mexico but bottled in the United States. Your guests will never know the difference. Mainly because there isn't any difference.

Also notice that the *platas* didn't score well. No matter how expensive or what percent of blue agave it contains, clear tequila always tastes harsher. Of course, there are those who would say that the *platas* have the vegetal sort of taste that tequila should have and that the *añejos* are an entirely different drink, a fine liquor to be sipped like cognac. We prefer a *reposado* or *añejo* when we are drinking tequila straight, but we often use a *plata* for margaritas.

We usually chase tequila shots with beer, but the salt-and-lime ritual is fun, too. Most people lick the back of their hand, shake a little salt on the wet spot, and then eat the salt, drink the shot, and bite into a lime wedge. There are many variations, including licking the salt off your lover's neck. But let's not get into how consenting adults drink tequila in private.

When company comes, the classy way to chase tequila is with a shot of sangrita, an orange-juice-and-chile concoction that is the most popular tequila chaser in Mexico. Tequila and sangrita are traditionally served in two identical tall shot glasses. La Viuda Sanchez is a popular brand that we see in many liquor stores, but if you can't find it, sangrita is easy enough to make.

Sangrita:

In a jar or bottle, combine 1/2 cup orange juice, 1/4 cup tomato juice, 1/4 cup fresh lime juice, 1 teaspoon minced serrano chile or 1 tablespoon pepper sauce, 1/2 teaspoon salt, and 2 tablespoons hibiscus syrup (page 25). Mix well and chill.

MARGARITAS

Some say it was a San Antonio society dame, Mrs. William (Margarita) Sames, who first served Margarita's cocktail at a party in 1948. Others insist it was bartender Francisco "Pancho" Morales of Juarez who accidentally concocted the drink on July 4, 1942, while trying to make something else.

Whichever side of the border it was invented on, the margarita is the quintessential Tex-Mex cocktail. And like so many popular Tex-Mex creations, it has suffered greatly over the years at the hands of those who have tried to make it cheaper and more convenient. When you order a frozen margarita in a bar these days, you are almost certain to get rotgut tequila blended with a commercial margarita mix, frozen in a soft-serve machine.

These lemonade-flavored slushies are a sorry excuse for the real thing. The original recipe calls for fresh-squeezed lime juice, tequila, and orange liqueur. It's very sour and very strong. A few truly innovative bartenders have come up with some great variations over the years. Soaking prickly pear fruits in a jar of tequila and then mixing the pureed fruit with the red-tinted tequila to make a blood-red cactus margarita is one of the best new ideas we've seen. Mango puree is another great margarita mixer.

Purists like Pancho Morales and the other bartenders of Juarez think all these fruity margaritas are for kooks. We understand their loyalty to the original recipe. We also realize that the classic margarita is too sour and too strong for a lot of people. So we'll give you the original recipe and a couple of the kooky fruit recipes, too.

What constitutes a good margarita is controversial. Some people like them daiquiri style, sweet and fruity with the barest hint of tequila flavor. Others insist on a strong tequila taste gently tempered by citrus. Some like them frozen, some like them on the rocks. So be prepared to customize these recipes to your own taste and the tastes of your drinking companions.

Original Margarita

MEXICAN AND KEY LIMES ARE THE LITTLE ONES. IF YOU SUBSTITUTE PERSIAN LIMES (THE BIG ONES), YOU'LL NEED ONLY HALF A LIME. THIS IS A VERY STRONG COCKTAIL. IT SHOULD BE TREATED LIKE A MARTINI.

FILL A SHAKER GLASS with crushed ice and squeeze the lime juice into it. Wet the rim of two 4-ounce cocktail glasses with what's left of the lime. Dump a little salt on a dish towel and spin the moistened glass rims in it. Shake off the excess salt. Add the tequila and Cointreau to the shaker glass. Shake the cocktails with the ice and strain into the glasses, pouring carefully to avoid messing up the salted rims.

CRUSHED ICE

JUICE OF 1 MEXICAN OR KEY LIME

4 SHOTS (4 OUNCES) TEQUILA *PLATA*

2 SHOTS (2 OUNCES) COINTREAU

SALT

SERVES **2** PEOPLE

Jeffrey's Mandaritas

THIS IS ONE OF THE MOST POPULAR MARGARITAS AT JEFFREY'S RESTAURANT IN AUSTIN. THEY MAKE THEIR OWN TANGERINE SORBET, BUT STORE-BOUGHT WILL DO JUST FINE.

2 SHOTS (2 OUNCES) TEQUILA

1 SHOT (1 OUNCE) MANDARINE NAPOLEON OR COINTREAU

JUICE OF $\frac{1}{2}$ LIME

1 CUP TANGERINE SORBET

2 SLICES LIME

SERVES 2 PEOPLE

COMBINE ALL THE INGREDIENTS except the lime slices in a blender and blend until slushy. Serve in large martini glasses. Garnish each glass with a lime slice.

Hibiscus Margaritas

HIBISCUS IS KNOWN AS *JAMAICA* IN MEXICO. HIBISCUS SYRUP MIXED WITH WATER AND ICE IS A POPULAR SUMMER SOFT DRINK KNOWN AS *AGUA FRESCA DE JAMAICA* (PAGE 25). WE'VE USED THE HIBISCUS SYRUP HERE TO MAKE A TART, REFRESHING RED MARGARITA.

COMBINE THE TEQUILA, Cointreau, hibiscus syrup, lime juice, and ice in a blender and blend until slushy. Serve in large martini glasses. Garnish each glass with an orange slice.

2 SHOTS (2 OUNCES) TEQUILA

1 SHOT (1 OUNCE) COINTREAU

2 SHOTS (2 OUNCES) HIBISCUS SYRUP
(PAGE 25)

JUICE OF ½ LIME

1 CUP CRUSHED ICE

ORANGE SLICES
FOR GARNISH

SERVES 2 PEOPLE

Mango-Key Lime Margaritas

THIS TROPICAL MARGARITA IS MUCH FRUITIER AND EASIER TO DRINK THAN THE ORIGINAL. WE LIKE IT FROZEN, SO THE RECIPE CALLS FOR CRUSHED ICE. IF FROZEN DRINKS GIVE YOU HEADACHES, OMIT THE CRUSHED ICE AND SERVE IT ON THE ROCKS.

COMBINE THE TEQUILA, Cointreau, mango, orange juice, lime juice, and ice in a blender and blend until slushy. Serve in large martini glasses. Garnish each glass with a lime slice.

2 SHOTS (2 OUNCES) TEQUILA

1 SHOT (1 OUNCE) COINTREAU

$1/4$ FRESH MANGO
PEELED AND CHOPPED

$1/2$ CUP FRESH ORANGE JUICE

JUICE OF $1/2$ MEXICAN OR KEY LIME

1 CUP CRUSHED ICE

2 MEXICAN OR KEY LIME SLICES
FOR GARNISH

SERVES 2 PEOPLE

Jay McCarthy's Cactus 'Ritas

CHEF JAY McCARTHY INVENTED THIS DRINK WHILE HE WAS TRYING TO FIND A DECORATIVE USE FOR SOME LARGE GLASS BOTTLES. THE BLOOD RED TEQUILA WITH PRICKLY PEAR FRUIT NOT ONLY LOOKS GREAT IN THE BOTTLE, IT ALSO MAKES THE MOST STRIKING-LOOKING MARGARITA WE HAVE EVER SEEN. AND THE FLAVOR IS THE PERFECT BALANCE OF TART AND SWEET. AT THE ZUNI GRILL ON SAN ANTONIO'S RIVER WALK WHERE JAY CONCOCTED THIS DRINK, THEY HAVE SOLD AS MANY AS FIFTEEN HUNDRED IN A DAY.

10 LARGE, PURPLE PRICKLY PEAR FRUITS

1 BOTTLE (750 ML) TEQUILA *PLATA*

CRUSHED ICE

1/2 BOTTLE (1 1/2 CUPS) COINTREAU

10 LIMES

SERVES **10** PEOPLE

PEEL EACH PRICKLY PEAR FRUIT and put the peeled fruits in a large glass jar. Pour in the tequila so that the fruits are completely submerged. Seal tightly and allow to sit for 3 to 4 days.

For each margarita, remove 1 prickly pear fruit. To remove the seeds, mash the flesh through a large-mesh strainer into a bowl. Discard the seeds.

Put the strained fruit into a blender. Add 1/2 cup crushed ice, 2 shots (2 ounces) of the prickly pear–flavored tequila, 1 shot (1 ounce) Cointreau, and the juice of 1 lime. Blend until slushy and serve in a large martini glass.

Bloody Maria

TEQUILA IS A GREAT ALTERNATIVE TO GIN OR VODKA IN YOUR MORNING LIBATION, ESPECIALLY IF IT HAPPENS TO BE THE HAIR OF THE DOG THAT BIT YOU.

CRUSHED ICE

2 SHOTS (2 OUNCES) OF YOUR FAVORITE BREAKFAST TEQUILA

1 CUP TOMATO JUICE

JUICE OF 1/2 MEXICAN OR KEY LIME

DASH OF WORCESTERSHIRE SAUCE

FRESHLY GROUND BLACK PEPPER

2 CELERY STALKS

FAVORITE HOT-PEPPER SAUCE

SERVES 2 PEOPLE

FILL A SHAKER GLASS with crushed ice. Add the tequila, tomato juice, lime juice, Worcestershire sauce, and ground pepper to taste. Shake well. Pour into tall cocktail glasses filled with crushed ice, and garnish each glass with a celery stalk. Let imbibers add hot sauce to taste.

Angela's Tequila Toddy

ANGELA HAS BEEN BABYSITTING FOR OUR CHILDREN FOR
YEARS. SHE COMES FROM NICARAGUA, WHERE SHE CLAIMS
THAT THIS DRINK IS WIDELY ACKNOWLEDGED AS THE CURE
FOR THE COMMON COLD. WHETHER YOU FEEL SICK OR NOT,
THIS IS A GREAT NIGHTCAP ON A WINTER EVENING.

POUR THE MILK INTO A MUG until it is three-fourths full. Then pour the milk into a small saucepan and add all the spices. Warm over medium heat for 5 minutes, or until the milk steams a little. Put the sugar in the bottom of the mug, then strain the milk through a sieve back into the mug. Add the tequila. Drink hot.

MILK

1 CINNAMON STICK

1 WHOLE CLOVE

1 WHOLE STAR ANISE

1 TEASPOON SUGAR

1 SHOT (1 OUNCE) TEQUILA OF CHOICE

SERVES 1 PERSON

Agua Fresca de Jamaica

AGUA FRESCAS ARE FLAVORED WATERS, JUST LIKE LEMON-ADE. THEY MAKE GREAT KIDS' DRINKS AND WELCOME THIRST QUENCHERS ON A HOT DAY. MAKE THE HIBISCUS SYRUP IN ADVANCE AND KEEP IT IN THE REFRIGERATOR.

TO MAKE HIBISCUS SYRUP:

In a small saucepan, combine the water, hibiscus flowers, and sugar. Bring to a simmer over low heat, stirring to dissolve the sugar, then simmer for 10 minutes, or until reduced to 1½ cups. Pour through a fine-mesh strainer, let cool, and store in a tightly capped bottle or jar in the refrigerator for up to 1 week.

TO MAKE EACH DRINK:

Mix 2 or 3 tablespoons of syrup with water and ice in an 8-ounce glass.

1 CUP WATER

½ CUP DRIED HIBISCUS FLOWERS

½ CUP SUGAR

Serious Salsas

hOT SaUCEs aNd PePpER REliShES

CHAPTER 2

NEW MEXICO HAS ITS GREEN CHILES AND LOUISIANA HAS ITS SHAKER-BOTTLE SAUCES, BUT THE HOT-SAUCE CAPITAL OF THE UNITED

States is Texas. It was Tex-Mex food that made picante sauce popular in this country. Of course, we got all of our recipes from Mexico, but something happened in the translation. We ended up turning Mexican table sauce into a chip dip. If you've ever been to interior Mexico, you may have noticed that, except for tourist joints, restaurants there hardly ever serve a basket of tortilla chips with a bowl of hot sauce before your meal. Tortilla chips dunked in hot sauce is a Tex-Mex invention. But our loyalty to the tradition now borders on the fanatical. When Austin's Fonda San Miguel, an upscale interior-Mexican restaurant, attempted to do away with the chips and salsa before dinner because it wasn't authentically Mexican, their patrons protested vehemently. They finally had to relent to quell the revolt. Chips and hot sauce are the Tex-Mex equivalent of bread and butter. When you go to a restaurant, you expect them to be on the table, you expect them to be good, and you don't expect to pay for them.

We eat so much hot sauce in Texas that many Tex-Mex restaurants have made their reputation on the quality of their salsas alone. Home cooks are justly proud of their family recipes, too. In 1991, we started a friendly little contest in Austin to see who really made the best hot sauce. The response was overwhelming. Judging the Austin Hot Sauce Festival, as the event is now known, requires us to sample over three hundred salsas every year. In the process, we've had a chance to taste just about every combination of salsa ingredients imaginable.

One of the first questions the contest had to answer was about nomenclature: What's the difference between hot sauce, salsa, and pepper sauce? By our definition, pepper sauce is something that comes in a shaker bottle with the peppers suspended in a liquid, usually vinegar. When we say hot sauce, we mean the traditional Mexican table sauce also known as *salsa picante*. Sometimes hot sauce is cooked or made with some cooked ingredients. When all the ingredients are uncooked and coarsely chopped, we usually call it *pico de gallo*.

Salsa is a little tougher to keep tied down. The word means sauce in Spanish and used to be synonymous with plain old hot sauce. Lately though, salsa has slipped through the fence and started cavorting in faraway pastures. Caribbean sauces that combine tropical fruits, peppers, and other savory ingredients are also called salsas now. So are relishes made with mint, ginger, tamarind, and other nontraditional ingredients. Some of them are exceptionally good with grilled meats and fish dishes, so even though they don't go very well with tortilla chips, we are happy to stretch our definition of salsa to include them here.

The original Tex-Mex salsa evolved from the *molcajete* sauce of northern Mexico. A *molcajete* is a mortar made of coarse stone. The traditional recipe calls for chiles and tomatoes and sometimes garlic to be roasted in a *comal*, a flat cast-iron griddle, and then ground together in the *molcajete* with a *tejolote*, or pestle. Chopped onion soaked in lime juice and chopped cilantro are added along with salt to taste. This is a good basic recipe for hot sauce. You can use a food processor instead of the *molcajete*, but don't skip the roasting step. You'll be amazed at how much it improves the flavor. You can add a wonderful smoky flavor to the basic Tex-Mex hot sauce by using chipotles instead of fresh jalapeños or by smoking the tomatoes in a backyard smoker.

The other Tex-Mex classic is *salsa verde*, or "green sauce." It is made with tomatillos instead of tomatoes, and it has a refreshing tartness. *Salsa verde* is less common than the red stuff as a tortilla dunking sauce, but it doubles as an enchilada sauce that is the favorite with poultry dishes.

Just because you see a lot of unusual salsa recipes in this chapter, don't be deceived into thinking that we use them more often than old-fashioned picante sauce. We'll whip up a tropical fruit salsa to go with a particular dish once in a while. But we put a little bowl of picante sauce on the table for every meal. Designer salsas come and go, but classic picante sauce is like a little black dress. It never goes out of style.

Picante Sauce

CALIENTE IS THE SPANISH WORD FOR HOT, AS IN PIPING HOT. *PICANTE* IS THE SPANISH WORD FOR HOT, AS IN SPICY HOT. PICANTE COMES FROM THE VERB *PICAR*, WHICH MEANS TO BITE OR TO STING. IN SPANISH, YOU WOULD SAY, *"EL JALAPEÑO PICA MUCHO,"* WHICH LITERALLY MEANS, "THE JALAPEÑO STINGS A LOT." AS THE NAME IMPLIES, PICANTE SAUCE IS SUPPOSED TO BE FIERY. • THIS RECIPE IS THE MODERN VERSION OF OLD-FASHIONED *MOLCAJETE* SAUCE. IT IS ONE OF OUR FAVORITE EVERYDAY TABLE SAUCES, AND IT TASTES GREAT ON EGGS, CHIPS, TACOS, OR ALMOST ANYTHING. THE ROASTING STEP ADDS DEPTH TO THE FLAVOR. SOAKING THE ONIONS IN THE LIME JUICE AND SALT "COOKS" THEM AND REMOVES SOME OF THEIR BITTERNESS.

IN A SMALL BOWL, soak the onion in the lime juice for 15 minutes. Meanwhile, in a skillet over high heat, roast the tomatoes, jalapeño halves, and garlic clove, turning as needed, until slightly charred on all sides. Transfer the contents of the skillet to a blender and puree for 10 seconds or so; the mixture should remain chunky.

Transfer the puree to a bowl and add the onion and lime juice and the cilantro. Season to taste with salt. Use immediately, or cover and store refrigerated for up to 1 week.

½ ONION
FINELY DICED

1½ TABLESPOONS FRESH LIME JUICE

6 ROMA TOMATOES

2 JALAPEÑO CHILES
STEMMED, SEEDED, AND
HALVED LENGTHWISE

1 CLOVE GARLIC

1 CUP CHOPPED FRESH CILANTRO

SALT

MAKES 3 CUPS

Papaya-Habanero Salsa

THIS A GREAT MARINADE BECAUSE PAPAIN, AN ENZYME PRESENT IN PAPAYA, IS A NATURAL MEAT TENDERIZER. WE USE THE SALSA TO MARINATE FAJITAS, BUT IT ALSO TASTES GREAT WITH LOBSTER, CRAB, AND SHRIMP DISHES.

1 RIPE PAPAYA
HALVED, SEEDED, AND PEELED

$1/2$ HABANERO CHILE
SEEDED AND MINCED

$1/4$ TEASPOON SUGAR

2 TABLESPOONS FRESH LEMON JUICE

1 TABLESPOON OLIVE OIL

1 YELLOW TOMATO
SEEDED AND FINELY DICED

1 RED BELL PEPPER
ROASTED, PEELED, STEMMED, SEEDED, AND FINELY DICED (SEE PAGE 143)

$1/2$ CUP COARSELY CHOPPED FRESH CILANTRO

1 TABLESPOON MINCED FRESH MINT

SALT

MAKES **$2\frac{1}{2}$~3** CUPS

DICE HALF OF THE PAPAYA and set it aside. Cut up the other half, place in a blender, and add the habanero chile, sugar, lemon juice, and olive oil. Puree until smooth. Transfer the puree to a nonreactive bowl and add the reserved diced papaya, tomato, bell pepper, cilantro, and mint. Mix well and season to taste with salt. Let stand for 15 minutes to allow the flavors to blend before serving.

Green Sauce

A *SALSA VERDE* IS USUALLY MADE WITH TOMATILLOS, ONIONS, AND FRESH CHILES. THIS MORE ELABORATE AND FLAVORFUL GREEN SAUCE WAS INVENTED BY BRUCE AUDEN, OF BIGA IN SAN ANTONIO. HE SOMETIMES SERVES IT THERE ON CHICKEN STUFFED WITH CHEESE. WE USE IT WARM AS A SAUCE FOR ENCHILADAS AND OTHER COOKED DISHES AND CHILLED FOR CHIPS AND TACOS.

IN A MEDIUM-SIZED SKILLET, heat the olive oil over high heat. Add the garlic, serranos, scallions, and tomatillos and cook, stirring occasionally, for 4 to 6 minutes, or until the tomatillos start to discolor slightly. Deglaze with the wine, stirring to dissolve any browned bits, and bring to a boil. Boil for 30 seconds.

Transfer the contents of the skillet to a blender, add the poblano chiles and cilantro, and puree until smooth. Season to taste with salt. Use immediately as a sauce for cooked dishes, or chill and serve as a table sauce. It will keep, tightly capped, in the refrigerator for up to 1 day.

1 TABLESPOON OLIVE OIL

3 CLOVES GARLIC
HALVED

2 SERRANO CHILES
STEMMED AND MINCED

6 SCALLIONS
CHOPPED

6 TOMATILLOS
HUSKED AND QUARTERED

1 CUP DRY WHITE WINE

3 POBLANO CHILES
ROASTED, PEELED, STEMMED, AND SEEDED (SEE PAGE 142)

1 CUP CHOPPED FRESH CILANTRO

SALT

MAKES $1\frac{1}{2}$~2 CUPS

Ancho-Tomatillo Sauce

HERE'S ANOTHER TOMATILLO SAUCE, BUT THIS ONE ISN'T GREEN. THE ANCHO PEPPERS TURN IT SORT OF BROWN. IT'S ONE OF THE TASTIEST TOMATILLO SAUCES OF ALL, HOWEVER. THE ANCHO-TOMATILLO COMBINATION WAS INSPIRED BY MEXICAN COOKING AUTHORITY PATRICIA QUINTANA. USE IT AS A SAUCE FOR ENCHILADAS OR OTHER COOKED DISHES, OR SERVE CHILLED AS A TABLE SAUCE.

4 TABLESPOONS OLIVE OIL

¹/₂ ONION
THINLY SLICED

1 SERRANO CHILE
STEMMED AND MINCED

1 GARLIC CLOVE
MINCED

6 TOMATILLOS
HUSKED AND QUARTERED

2 ANCHO CHILES
STEMMED AND SEEDED

2 GUAJILLO CHILES
STEMMED AND SEEDED

1 TABLESPOON FRESH LEMON JUICE

¹/₄ CUP CHICKEN STOCK

1 CUP CHOPPED FRESH CILANTRO

SALT

MAKES **2** CUPS

IN A MEDIUM-SIZED SKILLET, heat 2 tablespoons of the olive oil over medium heat. Add the onion and cook, stirring, for about 6 minutes, or until light brown. Add the serrano, garlic, tomatillos, anchos, guajillos, lemon juice, and chicken stock. Reduce the heat to low and simmer for 5 to 7 minutes, or until the chiles are soft.

Transfer the contents of the skillet to a blender, add the cilantro, and puree until smooth. Strain through a sieve into a bowl and season to taste with salt.

In another medium-sized skillet over high heat, heat the remaining 2 tablespoons olive oil and carefully pour in the strained sauce. Cook for 1 to 2 minutes, or until it comes to a boil. Use immediately as a sauce for cooked dishes, or chill and serve as a table sauce. It will keep, tightly capped, in the refrigerator for up to 1 week.

Pico de Gallo

PICO DE GALLO, LITERALLY "ROOSTER'S BEAK," IS A POPULAR NAME FOR A COARSELY CHOPPED SALSA. THERE ARE MANY EXPLANATIONS FOR THE NAME. SOME SAY IT DESCRIBES THE SIMILARITY BETWEEN THE CHOPPING SOUND OF THE CHEF'S KNIFE AND THE PECKING OF A CHICKEN. OTHERS SAY IT DESCRIBES THE FEELING OF HAVING YOUR TONGUE PECKED BY A ROOSTER BECAUSE THE CHILE IS SO HOT.

1 CUP DICED TOMATO

1/2 CUP DICED ONION

1 SERRANO CHILE
STEMMED AND MINCED

1/4 CUP CHOPPED FRESH CILANTRO

1 TABLESPOON FRESH LEMON JUICE

SALT

MAKES 1¼ CUPS

COMBINE ALL THE INGREDIENTS in a bowl, including salt to taste. Mix well and refrigerate for 15 minutes to allow the flavors to blend before serving.

Pineapple Pico

THIS IS A SWEET-HOT VARIATION ON CLASSIC *PICO DE GALLO*. IT'S A SUMMERY SALSA THAT GOES WELL WITH GRILLED PORK OR SHRIMP.

COMBINE ALL THE INGREDIENTS in a bowl, including salt to taste. Mix well and refrigerate for 15 minutes to allow the flavors to blend before serving.

¹/₄ ONION
DICED

1 LARGE TOMATO
SEEDED AND DICED

1 CUP DICED PINEAPPLE

¹/₂ CUP CHOPPED FRESH CILANTRO

1 TEASPOON MINCED HABANERO
CHILE OR 1 TABLESPOON
HABANERO PEPPER SAUCE

2 TABLESPOONS FRESH LIME JUICE

SALT

MAKES 2¹/₂ CUPS

Mushroom Salsa

AS THEY COOK, MUSHROOMS PICK UP THE FLAVORS OF THE OTHER INGREDIENTS IN THE PAN. THE TRADITIONAL MEXICAN COMBINATION OF MUSHROOMS AND CHILES TAKES ADVANTAGE OF THIS FACT TO CREATE EARTHY MUSHROOM RELISHES LIKE THIS ONE. IF YOU LIKE MUSHROOMS, YOU'LL WANT PLENTY OF THIS SALSA ON YOUR GRILLED STEAKS OR SCRAMBLED EGG TACOS.

2 TABLESPOONS OLIVE OIL

3 PORTOBELLO MUSHROOMS
STEMMED AND DICED

2 SERRANO CHILES
STEMMED AND FINELY DICED

¼ CUP DRY WHITE WINE

2 TABLESPOONS FRESH LEMON JUICE

1 POBLANO CHILE
ROASTED, PEELED, STEMMED, SEEDED, AND DICED (SEE PAGE 142)

2 TABLESPOONS CHOPPED FRESH BASIL

SALT

MAKES **3** CUPS

IN A SKILLET, heat the olive oil over medium heat. Add the mushrooms and serranos. Cook, stirring, for 5 to 7 minutes, or until slightly soft. Add the wine and lemon juice and cook for 1 minute. Remove from the heat and transfer ¾ cup of the mushroom mixture to a blender. Puree until smooth.

Pass the puree through a sieve back into the skillet. Add the poblano chile, basil, and salt and stir well. Serve warm. This can be kept in the refrigerator for up to 4 days and reheated.

Corn Salsa

MEXICAN MARIGOLD MINT GROWS WILD IN TEXAS, WHERE IT IS ALSO KNOWN AS TEXAS TARRAGON. IT TASTES GREAT IN THIS RECIPE, BUT IF YOU CAN'T FIND ANY, DON'T DESPAIR. CONVENTIONAL TARRAGON WILL DO FINE. SERVE THIS SALSA ON GRILLED FISH AND CHICKEN.

IN A SMALL BOWL, soak the onion in the lime juice for 15 minutes. In a medium-sized skillet, heat the olive oil over low heat. Add the corn and sauté for 3 minutes, or until lightly cooked. Remove from the heat and allow to cool.

In a bowl, toss together the cooled corn, jicama, onion and lime juice, ground guajillo, Mexican marigold mint, and salt. Refrigerate for 15 minutes to allow the flavors to blend before serving.

1/2 CUP DICED PURPLE ONION

2 TABLESPOONS FRESH LIME JUICE

1 TABLESPOON OLIVE OIL

KERNELS CUT FROM 1 EAR OF CORN

1 CUP DICED JICAMA

1 GUAJILLO CHILE
GROUND TO A POWDER (SEE PAGE 143)

2 TABLESPOONS CHOPPED FRESH
MEXICAN MARIGOLD MINT OR TARRAGON

1/4 TEASPOON SEA SALT

MAKES 3 CUPS

CHAPTER **3**

Nuevos Huevos

BrEAKfAsT aNd BrUNcH DiShES

HUEVOS AND HOT SAUCE – IT'S A BREAKFAST, IT'S A HANGOVER CURE, IT'S A LIFESTYLE. WHAT A CATHARTIC JOY IT IS, ON A BLEARY-EYED morning, to make a happy face with two sunny-side up eggs for eyes and bacon strips for a mouth, and to douse that cheerful bastard with a torrent of fiery red sauce. 🐃 Then it's time to savor the delicious contrast — the yin of the warm, bland, and nurturing eggs, the yang of the fiery, acidic salsa. Is this a cosmic balance, or what? And, as if the eggs-and-hot-sauce combination wasn't already perfect, there are the countless permutations to consider: refried beans, warm tortillas, fried potatoes, a thick pork chop — it's hard to think of anything that doesn't go well with eggs and hot sauce. 🐂 There are tropical variations on the theme, like *huevos motuleños* served with habanero salsa and fried plantains, and Nuevo Tex-Mex versions of old-time favorites, such as *huevos Benedictos* made with chipotle hollandaise. And then there are breakfast tacos and migas, two Tex-Mex breakfasts that evolved out of modern realities.

Breakfast tacos are a Tex-Mex breakfast-to-go, a shining example of the American genius in the field of automotive cuisine. You can pull into a taco stand and grab a couple of these warm flour tortillas wrapped around your favorite breakfast-food fillings and still get to work on time. The typical list of filling choices includes eggs, bacon, sausage, refried beans, cheese, potatoes, tomatoes, and, of course, hot sauce. The taco is then consumed in your car or at your desk without the need for a fork, knife, or plate.

Migas are another breakfast dish that necessity invented. In this case, it was the necessity of doing something with leftover tortilla chips. The custom of serving chips and salsa to every customer in Tex-Mex restaurants creates an enormous inventory of chips. Unfortunately, they go stale quickly. How to use up the marginal chips is a challenge that was solved with *migas*.

Migas closely resemble one version of the Mexican dish *chilaquiles*, in which tortilla scraps are cooked with scrambled eggs. Tex-Mex restaurants substituted leftover chips and changed the name. The word *migas* means "crumbs" in Spanish. *Hacer migas* means to smash something to bits. And that's exactly what you do to tortilla chips to make *migas*.

Here are a few of our favorite ways to eat eggs and chiles — the breakfast that rebalances your cosmos.

Bacon-Gruyère Migas

THIS IS A RICH-TASTING REMAKE OF THE TEX-MEX CRUSHED-CHIP CLASSIC. TWO SERRANOS WILL MAKE THIS DISH PRETTY HOT. IF YOU'RE COOKING FOR KIDS AND ADULTS AT THE SAME TIME, YOU CAN CUT THE PEPPERS AND THEN LET THE ADULTS SEASON THEIR MIGAS WITH HOT SAUCE AT THE TABLE. SERVE WITH WHITE BEAN REFRITO (PAGE 119).

2 TABLESPOONS VEGETABLE OIL

2 CUPS TORTILLA CHIPS
LIGHTLY CRUSHED BY HAND

1 ONION
DICED

4 SLICES BACON
FRIED CRISP AND CRUMBLED

1 TOMATO
SEEDED AND DICED

2 SERRANO CHILES
STEMMED AND MINCED

8 EGGS

2 TABLESPOONS MILK

SALT

8 OUNCES GRUYÈRE CHEESE
GRATED

SERVES **4** PEOPLE

IN A MEDIUM-SIZED SKILLET, heat the oil over medium heat. Add the chips and cook, stirring, for 2 minutes, or until they start to brown. Add the onion, bacon, tomato, and chiles and cook, stirring, for 2 minutes, or until the onion is slightly cooked.

In a bowl, lightly beat the eggs, and then beat in the milk. Slowly add the beaten eggs to the pan, stirring and folding the eggs up from the bottom for 4 to 6 minutes, or until they are cooked to taste. Season with salt.

Divide the migas among 4 flameproof serving plates and top with the grated cheese, dividing it evenly. Slip each serving plate under a preheated broiler or in the microwave, and heat until the cheese is melted. Serve at once.

Chorizo Migas: Omit the vegetable oil and bacon. Sauté 8 ounces Mexican chorizos, removed from their casings and crumbled, over medium heat in the skillet for almost 5 minutes, or until well browned. Drain off all but 2 tablespoons of the fat and add the tortilla chips. Proceed as directed.

Mushroom Migas: Add 2 cups chopped fresh mushrooms to the oil before adding the tortilla chips and sauté for 3 minutes, or until soft. Proceed as directed.

Eggs in Hell

THIS DISH IS SORT OF LIKE HUEVOS RANCHEROS. BUT BASTING THE EGGS IN THE RANCHERO SAUCE KEEPS THEM TENDER LIKE POACHED EGGS AND CUTS DOWN ON THE FAT A LITTLE, TOO. SERVE WITH REFRIED BEANS, WARMED CORN TORTILLAS, AND, DEPENDING ON HOW YOUR MORNING IS GOING, HOT COFFEE OR COLD BEER.

PUREE THE TOMATOES IN A BLENDER; set aside. In a large skillet, heat the olive oil over medium heat. Add the jalapeño, onion, and bell pepper and sauté for 4 minutes, or until wilted. Add the tomato puree and bring to a boil. The sauce should be quite runny. If it is too solid, add a little water. Season to taste with salt.

Stir the sauce well and then gently break the eggs into the pan. Cover and allow to cook over medium heat for 4 minutes, or until the egg whites are well set but the yolks are still soft, or to desired doneness.

To serve, put 2 tortillas on each plate. Gently lift the eggs out of the pan and place one on each tortilla. Spoon the sauce around the eggs. Serve at once.

3 LARGE FRESH TOMATOES
CHOPPED, OR 1 CAN (15 OUNCES)
TOMATOES, DRAINED

2 TABLESPOONS OLIVE OIL

2 JALAPEÑO CHILES
STEMMED, SEEDED, AND MINCED

¹/₂ ONION
CHOPPED

¹/₂ GREEN BELL PEPPER
SEEDED AND CHOPPED

SALT

4 EGGS

4 CORN TORTILLAS
WARMED

SERVES **2** PEOPLE

Huevos Benedictos

HERE'S A SURPRISE FOR LOVERS OF EGGS BENEDICT: A NUEVO TEX-MEX VERSION WITH THE SMOKY HEAT OF CHIPOTLE CHILES IN THE HOLLANDAISE!

IN A BLENDER, combine the egg yolks, lemon juice, 1 tablespoon water, and chipotle puree. Turn the blender on briefly to mix. In a small saucepan, melt the butter over low heat until it starts to bubble. Turn the blender on and remove the inner part of the blender lid, if possible, or, failing that, remove the lid. With the blender motor running, gradually pour the hot melted butter onto the yolk mixture in a thin stream, processing until the mixture thickens. Season to taste with salt and set aside in a warm spot.

In a medium-sized skillet, fry the Canadian bacon over medium heat for 2 to 3 minutes on each side, or until hot. Set aside in a warm spot.

Meanwhile, bring the 4 cups water to a boil in a large, wide saucepan or deep skillet. Reduce the heat so the water gently simmers and add the vinegar. Crack 2 eggs into a shallow bowl. With a spoon, stir the simmering water in a circular motion to create a little whirlpool, and slide the raw eggs into the center of the eddy. Repeat with the remaining eggs. Poach the eggs for about 3 minutes, or until the whites are set and the yolks are still soft, or to desired doneness. Remove each egg with a slotted spoon and drain carefully on a paper towel.

Put 2 toasted muffin halves, split-side up, on each of 4 plates. Spread each half with the beans and then place a slice of Canadian bacon and a poached egg atop the beans. Top each egg with some of the hollandaise and garnish with the cilantro.

---

4 EGG YOLKS

1 TABLESPOON FRESH LEMON JUICE

1 TABLESPOON PLUS 4 CUPS WATER

2 TEASPOONS CHIPOTLE PUREE
(SEE PAGE 144)

1/2 CUP (1/4 POUND) UNSALTED BUTTER

SALT

4 THIN SLICES CANADIAN BACON

1/4 CUP WHITE WINE VINEGAR

8 EGGS

1 CUP BLACK BEAN AND PROSCIUTTO REFRITO
HEATED (PAGE 120)

4 ENGLISH MUFFINS
SPLIT AND TOASTED

1/2 CUP CHOPPED FRESH CILANTRO

SERVES 4 PEOPLE

Shown with Roasted Potatoes with Garlic and Mexican Oregano (page 126) and a Bloody Maria (page 22).

Spinach and Mushroom Chilaquiles

THIS IS A NONTRADITIONAL WAY TO MAKE A TRADITIONAL DISH. INSTEAD OF SAUTÉING THE INGREDIENTS, THEY ARE LAYERED AND BAKED. THINK OF IT AS MEXICAN BREAKFAST LASAGNA.

¼ CUP OLIVE OIL
OR AS NEEDED

12 CORN TORTILLAS
(A GREAT WAY TO USE UP STALE
OR BROKEN TORTILLAS)

1 POUND MUSHROOMS,
PREFERABLY PORTOBELLOS OR CRIMINI
STEMMED AND SLICED

4 CUPS SPINACH LEAVES
CHOPPED

SALT

2 CUPS DRAINED COOKED
WHITE BEANS (SEE PAGE 116)
OR CANNED WHITE BEANS

8 OUNCES JACK CHEESE
THINLY SLICED

GREEN SAUCE
(PAGE 31)

SERVES 4 PEOPLE

PREHEAT AN OVEN TO 300 DEGREES F. In a skillet, warm ¼ cup olive oil over low heat. Add the tortillas one at a time and cook for 15 seconds on each side. Transfer to paper towels to drain.

When all of the tortillas have been heated, there should be at least 2 tablespoons olive oil left in the skillet. If not, add oil as needed and place over medium heat. Add the mushrooms and cook, stirring, for 7 to 10 minutes, or until any liquid they have released has evaporated. Add the spinach and cook for 2 minutes longer, or until wilted. Season with salt and set aside.

Butter a 9-by-12-inch baking dish. Place 4 tortillas in the dish, covering the bottom completely and overlapping as necessary. Cover with one third of the spinach-mushroom mixture and one third of the white beans. Top with one third of the cheese slices and then one third of the sauce. Repeat the layers twice, ending with the sauce.

Bake for 20 minutes, or until heated through. Serve hot directly from the dish.

Serves 4 as a main dish, or 6 as a side dish.

Nuevos Huevos Motuleños

THE TINY YUCATÁN VILLAGE OF MOTUL USED TO BE FAMOUS FOR TWO THINGS — HENEQUEN AND ONE OF MEXICO'S BEST BREAKFAST DISHES, *HUEVOS MOTULEÑOS*. HENEQUEN IS A CACTUS FIBER THAT WAS ONCE USED TO MAKE THE FINEST ROPE IN THE WORLD. BUT SINCE THE INVENTION OF NYLON, THE FORMERLY LUCRATIVE HENEQUEN TRADE HAS ALL BUT DISAPPEARED. NOW, MOTUL'S ONLY CLAIM TO FAME IS BREAKFAST.

IN A LARGE SKILLET, melt the butter over medium heat. Break the eggs into the skillet and fry sunny-side up until done to your liking.

Meanwhile, place 2 teaspoonfuls of black beans on each of 4 plates. Put 2 chalupa shells on each plate, using the beans as an anchor. Divide the rest of the beans among the 8 shells, spreading the beans gently to avoid breaking them. Slide a fried egg onto each bean-covered chalupa shell, cover with the salsa, and top with the crumbled cheese. Garnish each plate with 4 slices of fried plantain. Serve at once.

Fried Plantains: Peel two very ripe plantains and slice into 1/2-inch slices. Melt 2 tablespoons of butter in a skillet and fry the plantain slices slowly, turning often for 10 minutes or until golden brown.

1 TABLESPOON BUTTER

8 EGGS

3 CUPS BLACK BEAN
AND PROSCIUTTO REFRITO
HEATED (PAGE 120)

8 FRESHLY FRIED CHALUPA SHELLS
(SEE PAGE 148)

1/2 CUP PAPAYA-HABANERO SALSA
(PAGE 30)

1 CUP CRUMBLED QUESO BLANCO OR
OTHER MILD WHITE CHEESE

SERVES 4 PEOPLE

Banana Cheese Omelet

HERE'S AN EGG DISH WITH NO HOT STUFF. IF YOU'RE MAKING THIS FOR KIDS, USE SOUR CREAM INSTEAD OF GOAT CHEESE.

---

3 EGGS

1 TABLESPOON MILK

PINCH OF SALT

2 TEASPOONS BUTTER

1 BANANA
PEELED AND
HALVED LENGTHWISE

2 TABLESPOONS FRESH GOAT CHEESE

**1/3 CUP SUGAR MIXED WITH
1 TEASPOON GROUND CINNAMON**

SERVES **1** PERSON

[OR 2 KIDS]

IN A BOWL, whisk together the eggs, milk, and salt. In a medium-sized nonstick skillet, melt the butter over low heat. Pour in the eggs and, using a wooden spatula, bring the eggs from the sides to the center of the pan, tilting the pan to get more egg mixture into the section you've emptied. Repeat this process until the eggs aren't runny anymore.

To fill the omelet, place the banana halves and goat cheese or sour cream atop one half of the eggs. Sprinkle two-thirds of the sugar-cinnamon mixture over the bananas and cheese and then fold the other side of the eggs over the toppings. Sprinkle the remaining cinnamon and sugar on top and serve hot.

Truffled Egg Tacos

EVERYBODY KNOWS HOW TO MAKE EGG TACOS; BUT HERE'S A VERSION YOU DON'T SEE EVERY DAY.

TO MAKE THE CREPES, in a nonreactive bowl, combine the cornmeal, milk, egg, and the 1 tablespoon melted butter. Whisk until a batter forms, and then let stand for 30 minutes.

Melt 1/4 teaspoon of the remaining butter in a 6-inch nonstick skillet over medium heat. When the butter starts to bubble, ladle about 2 tablespoons of the batter into the pan. It should spread to form a round about 5 inches in diameter. Cook for about 1 minute. Carefully turn the crepe over and cook for another minute, or until light brown. Transfer to a paper towel to drain, then set aside in a warm spot. Repeat using the remaining batter and butter to make 4 crepes in all.

Wipe out the skillet. To make the filling, melt the butter over low heat. Pour in the eggs and, using a spatula, push the eggs from the bottom to form long curds. Continue cooking in this manner until the eggs have a creamy, loose consistency; this should take 4 to 6 minutes. Season with salt.

Put 1 crepe on each plate. Divide the eggs among the crepes. Garnish with the truffle slices and chives. Serve the Mushroom Salsa on the side.

Salmon Roe–Egg Tacos: Omit the truffles and Mushroom Salsa. Top each mound of eggs with a heaping teaspoon of sour cream and a teaspoonful of salmon roe.

Wild Mushroom–Egg Tacos: Omit the truffles and Mushroom Salsa. Sauté 1 cup sliced wild mushrooms in 1 tablespoon olive oil for 3 minutes, or until tender. Season with salt. Add to the beaten eggs and cook as directed.

FOR THE BLUE CORNMEAL CREPES:

1/4 CUP BLUE CORNMEAL

1/4 CUP MILK

1 EGG
BEATEN

1 TABLESPOON BUTTER, MELTED AND COOLED, PLUS 1 TEASPOON FOR COOKING

SALT

FOR THE FILLING:

4 TEASPOONS BUTTER

6 EGGS
BEATEN

2 BLACK TRUFFLES (AVAILABLE AT SPECIALTY MARKETS)
THINLY SLICED

2 TABLESPOONS CHOPPED FRESH CHIVES

MUSHROOM SALSA
(PAGE 38)

SERVES **4** PEOPLE

The Taco Dichotomy

SoFT VeRSuS CrUNcHY

CHAPTER 4

TEX-MEX TACOS ARE CRUNCHY. MEXICAN TACOS DO NOT CRUNCH. THIS DICHOTOMY IS THE BIGGEST DIFFERENCE BETWEEN TEX-MEX and Mexican food. Mexicans don't care much about crunch. And on this side of the border, we are crunchaholics. ♪ Maybe Americans like crunchy foods because we crave stimulation. Maybe crunching relieves stress. Whatever the reason, Americans have had a long love affair with salty, crunchy foods. And Tex-Mex has played a huge role in that romance. ⚘ It could be argued that it was Fritos Corn Chips that first gave America a taste for Tex-Mex. They were formulated in San Antonio, Texas, in 1932, and by the late 1950s, the crunchy corn chips were well known across the country. Richard Nixon gave Nikita Khrushchev a bag in 1959. In the early 1960s, a company mascot called the Frito Kid appeared on the "Tonight Show" and persuaded Johnny Carson to try the chips and bean dip. Carson raved about the combination, and the new fad quickly swept the country. The heyday of Tex-Mex followed soon after.

When most Americans first met Tex-Mex, they saw it as a snack-food cuisine, and they found the concept enormously appealing. No wonder Tex-Mex took so much heat when the population became concerned about healthy eating. When the low-fat fad took off, Tex-Mex went into a slump.

Tex-Mex also missed out on the comfort-food trend. Crunchy tacos aren't one of those soothing dishes like meat loaf or mashed potatoes. Comfort foods are the opposite of crunchy snacks. You don't associate them with tequila shots or late-night parties. You think of them more as a great prelude to a nap. (Are we getting old, or what?)

But health concerns and soothing dishes have brought us around to the other extreme of the taco dichotomy. Crispy tacos are now making way for soft tortilla wraps. Nuevo Tex-Mex proposes finally to put an end to the old dichotomy. Whether they are crispy or soft, we still call them tacos. And we love them both.

Here then are the two branches of the taco dichotomy: loud, crispy tacos for those electric nights when you crave excitement, and soft, warm tacos for those quiet evenings when you want your dinner to sing you a lullaby. And if you're still locked into the beef, shredded lettuce, and grated cheese thing, then try a Nuevo Tex-Mex Steak, Endive, and Blue Cheese Taco. You'll never go back to the hamburger!

Steak, Endive, and Blue Cheese Tacos

HERE'S OUR TRIBUTE TO THE CLASSIC TEX-MEX TACO. IT'S GOT BEEF, LETTUCE, TOMATO, AND CHEESE — EVERYTHING YOU EXPECT — BUT WHAT A DIFFERENCE GOOD INGREDIENTS MAKE!

1¹/₂ TO 2 POUNDS RIB-EYE STEAKS

SALT AND FRESHLY GROUND
BLACK PEPPER

8 FRESHLY FRIED TACO SHELLS
(SEE PAGE 147)

2 HEADS BELGIAN ENDIVE
SLICED CROSSWISE

¹/₂ CUP CHOPPED YELLOW TOMATO

¹/₂ CUP CRUMBLED BLUE CHEESE,
PREFERABLY ROQUEFORT

PINEAPPLE PICO
(PAGE 35)

MAKES 8 TACOS

HEAT THE GRILL. Cut the rib-eye steaks into long, thin strips. Season the strips with salt and pepper.

Arrange the steak strips over a very hot fire and cook, turning once, for 4 to 6 minutes, or to desired doneness. Transfer the meat to a cutting board. Cut into easy-to-eat chunks.

Divide the meat among the 8 taco shells. Top each with an equal amount of the endive, tomatoes, blue cheese, and Pineapple Pico.

Variation: You can substitute queso fresco, feta, or any other crumbly cheese for the blue cheese.

Crispy Chicken Tacos

WE DEDICATE THIS RECIPE TO ROBERT AMAYA OF AMAYA'S TACO VILLAGE IN AUSTIN, HOME OF OUR FAVORITE OLD-FASHIONED CRISPY TACOS.

PREHEAT AN OVEN TO 350 DEGREES F. Place the chicken in a baking dish and top it with the onion, serrano chile, tomato, and beer. Sprinkle with salt to taste and cover with aluminum foil.

Bake for 8 to 10 minutes, or until cooked through. Transfer the chicken mixture to a bowl, add the salsa, and mix well. Divide the mixture among the 4 taco shells.

1 BONELESS, SKINLESS WHOLE CHICKEN BREAST, ABOUT 7 OUNCES
JULIENNED

1/4 ONION
JULIENNED

1 SERRANO CHILE
STEMMED AND MINCED

1 TOMATO
CHOPPED

1/2 CUP BEER

SALT

1 CUP MUSHROOM SALSA
(PAGE 38)

4 FRESHLY FRIED TACO SHELLS
(SEE PAGE 147)

MAKES 4 TACOS

Shark-BLT Tacos

SAN DIEGO, CALIFORNIA, MADE FISH TACOS FAMOUS. YOU CAN FIND THEM ALL OVER TOWN THERE. YOU CAN EVEN BUY THEM AT THE CONCESSION STAND AT JACK MURPHY STADIUM. THIS RECIPE DRESSES UP SOUTHERN CALIFORNIA FISH TACOS WITH THE DELICIOUS ADDITIONS OF BACON, LETTUCE, AND TOMATO. BUT IT'S THE MAYONNAISE THAT REALLY MAKES THE WHOLE THING SING. IF YOU DON'T HAVE TIME TO WHIP UP HABANERO MAYO FROM SCRATCH, CHEAT (SEE CHEATING TIPS INCLUDED WITH THE RECIPE), OR JUST TOP PLAIN MAYONNAISE WITH A SPOONFUL OF SALSA.

1 POUND VERY FRESH SHARK STEAKS
ABOUT ½ INCH THICK

1 ONION
CUT INTO ¼-INCH-THICK RINGS

2 TABLESPOONS OLIVE OIL

2 GUAJILLO CHILE POWDER
(SEE PAGE 143)

8 FRESHLY FRIED TACO SHELLS
(SEE PAGE 147)

4 SLICES BACON
FRIED CRISP AND CRUMBLED

1 HEAD SOFT LETTUCE, PREFERABLY BOSTON
CAREFULLY RINSED AND JULIENNED

1 TOMATO
SEEDED AND DICED

1 CUP HABANERO MAYO
(PAGE 71)

MAKES **8** TACOS

PREHEAT A BROILER. Place the shark steaks and onion rings on a broiler pan and coat evenly on both sides with the olive oil and guajillo chile powder. Place the pan under the broiler 6 inches from the heat and broil for 2 minutes. Turn over the shark steaks and onions and cook for 3 minutes longer, or until the steaks are just done and the onions are lightly charred. Do not overcook the fish, or it will be tough. Remove the pan from the broiler and cut the cooked shark into long strips, removing any skin or bones. Divide the shark meat and onion rings among the taco shells. Top with the bacon, lettuce, tomato, and Habanero Mayo.

Shrimp Chili Tacos

THIS SHRIMP CHILI IS SO GOOD, YOUR FRIENDS AND FAMILY WILL BE LUCKY IF THERE'S ANY LEFT TO PUT ON THE TACOS AT DINNERTIME. TRY TO CONTROL YOURSELF!

1 TABLESPOON OLIVE OIL

16 MEDIUM-SIZED SHRIMP
PEELED, DEVEINED, AND CUT INTO SMALL CHUNKS

1 ONION
DICED

2 TABLESPOONS ROASTED GARLIC PUREE
(SEE PAGE 145)

2 CUPS DICED, SEEDED TOMATOES

¼ CUP MINCED FRESH MEXICAN MARIGOLD MINT OR MARJORAM

2 TABLESPOONS CHIPOTLE PUREE
(SEE PAGE 144)

SALT

8 FRESHLY FRIED TACO SHELLS
(SEE PAGE 147)

1 CUP PAPAYA-HABANERO SALSA
(PAGE 30)

MAKES 8 TACOS

IN A MEDIUM-SIZED SKILLET, heat the olive oil over high heat. Add the shrimp and onion and sauté for 2 minutes, or until the shrimp are opaque. Add the garlic puree, tomatoes, marigold mint, and chipotle puree and cook for 1 minute. Season to taste with salt. Remove from the heat.

Divide the shrimp chili among the 8 taco shells. Garnish each taco with Papaya-Habanero Salsa.

Shrimp Chili Chalupas: Use the shrimp chili mixture as a topping for chalupas and garnish with a dollop of sour cream and Papaya-Habanero Salsa.

Shrimp Chili Nachos: If you ate too much of the shrimp chili to make tacos, put what's left on tortilla chips and call them nachos.

Chicken-Fried Tuna Tacos

OKAY, IT SOUNDS BIZARRE. BUT THINK ABOUT IT FOR A MINUTE. TUNA, RARE IN THE MIDDLE, WITH A PIPING-HOT, CRISPY CRUST, SLATHERED IN COLD CHILE-FLAVORED SOUR CREAM ON A CRUNCHY TACO WITH LETTUCE AND TOMATO. NOW GO BUY THE TUNA.

TO MAKE THE CHIPOTLE SOUR CREAM, in a small bowl, stir together the sour cream, chipotle puree, lemon juice, garlic puree, and salt to taste. Cover and chill until ready to use. You should have about 1 cup. (Sour cream lovers will want to put this on top of their enchiladas, their chalupas, and their nachos, too. And don't forget it when you make fajitas.)

Pour peanut oil into a medium-sized saucepan to a depth of 2 inches. Heat the peanut oil over high heat. Meanwhile, season the tuna fingers with salt and pepper. Put the flour in 1 shallow bowl and buttermilk in another. Dredge each tuna finger in the flour, dip it in the buttermilk, and dredge it in the flour again.

Just when the oil begins to smoke, carefully slip the tuna fingers into the saucepan. Cook, turning once, for 1 minute on each side, or until golden and just done. Drain briefly on paper towels. Place 1 tuna finger in each taco shell. Top with the lettuce, tomatoes, and the chipotle sour cream.

FOR THE CHIPOTLE SOUR CREAM:

$2/_3$ CUP SOUR CREAM

1 TABLESPOON CHIPOTLE PUREE
(SEE PAGE 144)

1 TABLESPOON FRESH LEMON JUICE

2 TABLESPOONS ROASTED GARLIC PUREE
(SEE PAGE 145)

SALT

FOR THE TACOS:

PEANUT OIL FOR FRYING

1 POUND VERY FRESH TUNA
CUT INTO 8 EQUAL-SIZED FINGERS

SALT AND FRESHLY GROUND BLACK PEPPER

ALL-PURPOSE FLOUR FOR DREDGING

BUTTERMILK FOR DREDGING

8 FRESHLY FRIED TACO SHELLS
(SEE PAGE 147)

1 HEAD SOFT LETTUCE, PREFERABLY BOSTON
CAREFULLY RINSED AND JULIENNED

1 CUP DICED, SEEDED TOMATOES
SEASONED WITH SALT

MAKES 8 TACOS

Crispy Pork, Guacamole, and Chili-Pecan Tacos

CHOPPED PECANS TOASTED WITH A COATING OF ANCHO CHILE GIVE A NUTTY ACCENT TO THE ALREADY WONDERFUL COMBINATION OF CRISPY PORK AND GUACAMOLE. THIS IS ONE OF OUR FAVORITES — A TRANSCENDENT SOFT-TACO EXPERIENCE. IT TASTES EVEN BETTER WITH "TWICE-COOKED PORK," SO REMEMBER THIS RECIPE WHEN YOU HAVE PORK LEFTOVERS.

1/4 CUP OLIVE OIL

1 1/2 POUNDS BONELESS PORK LOIN
THINLY SLICED

SALT

1 TABLESPOON BUTTER

1 CUP CHOPPED PECANS

1/4 CUP FINELY CHOPPED ANCHO CHILE

2 CUPS NUEVO GUACAMOLE
(PAGE 78)

8 FLOUR TORTILLAS
WARMED

MAKES 8 TACOS

IN A MEDIUM-SIZED SKILLET, heat the olive oil over high heat. Meanwhile, season the pork with salt. When the oil is hot, add the pork in batches and sear on both sides for 5 to 7 minutes, or until very crisp. Transfer the pork to a cutting board, cut into narrow strips, and keep warm.

In a small skillet, melt the butter over low heat. Add the pecans and ancho chile and cook for 3 to 5 minutes, or until the butter starts turning reddish brown. Season with salt. Transfer to a serving bowl.

Spoon 1/4 cup guacamole onto each tortilla, divide the pork among the tortillas, and top each with some of the chilied pecans. Fold into a taco and serve.

Pot Roast Tacos

THIS RECIPE WAS INSPIRED BY THE CHILIED POT ROAST IN *JAMES BEARD'S AMERICAN COOKERY*. THE MEAT SHOULD BE COOKED UNTIL IT IS ABSOLUTELY FALLING APART. THE SOFT BEEF, CLOAKED IN THICK CHILE SAUCE AND WRAPPED IN FLOUR TORTILLAS, IS COMFORT FOOD AT ITS FINEST. TO MAKE THE POT ROAST MILD ENOUGH FOR THE WHOLE FAMILY, OMIT THE PASILLAS. ROASTED POTATOES WITH GARLIC AND MEXICAN OREGANO (PAGE 126) AND A GREEN SALAD GO WELL WITH THE TACOS.

"7 BONE" CHUCK ROAST, ABOUT 4 POUNDS

1 TABLESPOON SALT

1 TEASPOON FRESHLY GROUND BLACK PEPPER

2 CLOVES GARLIC
SLIVERED

2 TABLESPOONS VEGETABLE OIL

2 ONIONS
COARSELY CHOPPED

1 CUP BEEF STOCK

1 CUP TOMATO SAUCE

1 TEASPOON DRIED OREGANO

1/2 TEASPOON GROUND CUMIN

2 ANCHO CHILES
STEMMED AND SEEDED

2 PASILLA CHILES
STEMMED AND SEEDED (OPTIONAL)

12 WARM FLOUR TORTILLAS
WARMED

MAKES **12** TACOS

SEASON THE ROAST WITH THE SALT AND PEPPER. Pierce the meat with a knife in several places and insert the garlic slivers. In a large, heavy pot, heat the oil over high heat. Brown the roast for 3 minutes on each side, then add the onions. Cook, stirring occasionally, until the onions are tender, about 5 minutes. Add the stock, tomato sauce, oregano, and cumin. Reduce the heat to low.

Put the ancho and pasilla chiles in the braising liquid and allow to simmer for 10 minutes, or until soft. Remove the chiles and 1 cup of the braising liquid and transfer to a blender. Puree the mixture and return it to the pot. Cover and simmer over low heat for 3 to 4 hours, or until the meat falls completely from the bone and shreds easily with a fork.

Transfer the meat to a cutting board. Trim away the gristle and bones. Shred the meat and put it on a serving plate. Pour the braising liquid into a gravy boat or small bowl. Serve with the warm tortillas.

Tacos al Pastor

IN MEXICO CITY, THESE TACOS ARE MADE FROM SPICED PORK COOKED ON A ROTISSERIE. GÜERO'S TACO BAR IN AUSTIN HAS IMPORTED THE *TACO AL PASTOR* TRADITION FROM MEXICO CITY, ROTISSERIES AND ALL. GÜERO'S OWNERS, ROB AND CATHY LIPPINCOTT, GAVE US THIS RECIPE FOR MAKING THE TACOS AT HOME.

IN A MEDIUM-SIZED BOWL, combine the garlic, vinegar, oregano, guajillo chile powder, black pepper, cumin, salt to taste, orange juice, and achiote paste. Add the pork slices and turn to coat both sides. Marinate for at least 1 hour, and not more than 3 hours.

Heat the grill. Place the meat over a hot fire and cook, turning once and basting with any leftover marinade during cooking, until crisp. At the same time, grill the pineapple strips, turning as needed, until lightly browned. Both the pork and pineapple should take no longer than about 5 minutes.

To assemble, chop the grilled pork into ¼-inch pieces. Cut the pineapple into ½-inch pieces. Place the pork on the warmed tortillas and top with the onion, cilantro, and pineapple pieces. Serve the Picante Sauce on the side.

¼ CUP GRANULATED GARLIC

1 TABLESPOON CIDER VINEGAR

1 TEASPOON DRIED OREGANO

1 TEASPOON GUAJILLO CHILE POWDER
(SEE PAGE 143)

1 TEASPOON FRESHLY GROUND BLACK PEPPER

PINCH OF GROUND CUMIN

SALT

2 CUPS FRESH ORANGE JUICE

1½ TABLESPOONS ACHIOTE PASTE
(SEE PAGE 142)

2 POUNDS BONELESS PORK LOIN
THINLY SLICED

½ PINEAPPLE
PEELED, CORED, AND CUT INTO LONG, THICK STRIPS

12 CORN TORTILLAS
WARMED

1 ONION
FINELY CHOPPED

1 BUNCH FRESH CILANTRO
FINELY CHOPPED

PICANTE SAUCE
(PAGE 29)

MAKES **12** TACOS

CHAPTER

5

Fiesta Food

SnACKS aND ApPETiZErS

IF YOU HAVE A *BIG* APPETITE, YOU MIGHT CONSIDER A PILE OF STEAK NACHOS OR A STACK OF CRAB QUESADILLAS AS AN APPETIZER. BUT THE TRUTH is most of these snacks are pretty hearty. They come not from the French tradition of hors d'oeuvres but from the Mexican tradition of *antojitos*. ✹ Mexicans think of *antojitos* the way Americans think of hot dogs, hamburgers, or pizza slices. They aren't little bites, but they aren't serious meals either. They are treats you eat when you're on the go. *Tacos al pastor* from a rotisserie set up in the street, grilled steak and sizzling onion chalupas served at a bar — these are the true spirit of *antojitos*. They are fun foods, indulgences, fiesta treats.

Tex-Mex has put its own spin on this Mexican tradition. While Tex-Mex embraces quesadillas, chalupas, and other such party foods, the indigenous Tex-Mex snack is what we call nachos. A joint called the Victory Club in the border town of Piedras Negras claims to have invented nachos sometime during World War II. They were first served at the Texas State Fair in 1966, and began their decline in 1975, when they showed up on the concession-stand menu at a Texas Rangers baseball game in Arlington, Texas. Ever since then, a pile of corn chips in a paper dish dotted with pickled jalapeño slices and dribbled with orange cheese goop has become the standard rendition of nachos.

It doesn't have to be that way. Nachos can be exciting, exotic, extraordinary. If it makes you feel any better, call these nachos Nuevo Tex-Mex canapés. They're really just little treats you can pop into your mouth in one bite like any other canapé. You can make the recipes here with store-bought tortilla chips (the round ones are the sturdiest), or you can fry up your own chips using the method explained in Kitchen Notes (see page 148).

Sirloin Nachos

THIS RECIPE WAS A BIG AWARD-WINNER AT THE 1995 TEXAS HILL COUNTRY WINE AND FOOD FESTIVAL. DESPITE ITS FANCY PEDIGREE, IT'S STILL A GOOD WAY TO USE UP THOSE ODD HUNKS OF STEAK YOU BRING HOME IN A DOGGY BAG FROM THE STEAKHOUSE.

8 OUNCES BONELESS SIRLOIN STEAK

1 TABLESPOON GUAJILLO CHILE POWDER
(SEE PAGE 143)

1 TEASPOON FRESHLY
GROUND BLACK PEPPER

1 TEASPOON GARLIC POWDER

2 TABLESPOONS OLIVE OIL

16 NACHO CHIPS

1½ CUPS BLACK BEAN AND
PROSCIUTTO REFRITO
HEATED (PAGE 120)

½ CUP PINEAPPLE PICO
(PAGE 35)

½ CUP HABANERO MAYO
(PAGE 71)

MAKES **16** NACHOS

TRIM THE FAT FROM THE STEAK. Cut the steak against the grain into thin slices. Cut the sirloin slices again into medallions that are slightly smaller than the chips you're using. Lay the sirloin medallions on a flat surface. In a small bowl, combine the guajillo chile powder, black pepper, and garlic powder. Dust each medallion with a pinch of the dry mixture, turn, and dust the other side.

In a medium-sized skillet, heat the olive oil over medium heat. Cook the steak medallions for 1 minute on each side for medium-rare (or until just heated if you're using leftovers).

Assemble the nachos by spreading a spoonful of black beans on each chip and then placing a sirloin medallion on it. Top the sirloin with about a heaping teaspoonful of the Pineapple Pico and a heaping tea-spoon of the Habanero Mayo. Place on a serving plate and serve immediately.

Crab-and Spinach Nachos

A CRUNCHY CHIP TOPPED WITH HOT CREAMY SPINACH, LOTS OF CRABMEAT, AND MELTED GRUYÈRE IS OUR FAVORITE NACHO OF ALL TIME. MAKE PLENTY — THESE HAVE BEEN KNOWN TO TURN BLACK-TIE AFFAIRS INTO SHOVING MATCHES.

PREHEAT AN OVEN TO 375 DEGREES F. In a skillet, heat the 2 tablespoons olive oil over medium heat. Add the garlic and onion and sauté for 3 to 4 minutes, or until the onion is translucent. Add the spinach and mint and sauté for 2 to 4 minutes, or until the spinach is wilted. Remove from the heat and season with sea salt to taste.

Divide the spinach among the nacho chips. Put the crabmeat on top, dividing it evenly, and then sprinkle each chip with an equal amount of the cheese. Transfer to a baking sheet and bake for 5 to 7 minutes, or until the cheese is completely melted.

Transfer to a serving plate and garnish each nacho with a heaping teaspoonful of the salsa. Serve immediately.

2 TABLESPOONS PLUS 1/2 CUP OLIVE OIL

3 CLOVES GARLIC
MINCED

1/2 RED ONION
DICED

1/2 POUND SPINACH
CHOPPED

1 TABLESPOON MINCED FRESH MEXICAN MARIGOLD MINT OR TARRAGON

SEA SALT

16 NACHO CHIPS

8 OUNCES FRESH-COOKED CRABMEAT
PICKED OVER FOR SHELLS AND FLAKED

1 CUP GRATED GRUYÈRE OR COMTÉ CHEESE

1/2 CUP PAPAYA-HABANERO SALSA
(PAGE 30)

MAKES **16** NACHOS

Jeffrey's Oyster Nachos

JEFFREY'S RESTAURANT IN AUSTIN SELLS FORTY ORDERS OF THESE A DAY. EVEN PEOPLE WHO HAVE NEVER LIKED OYSTERS GO WILD FOR THIS CRISPY FRIED OYSTER ON A CRUNCHY CHIP.

CANOLA OIL FOR FRYING

BUTTERMILK FOR DREDGING

ALL-PURPOSE FLOUR FOR DREDGING

16 OYSTERS
SHUCKED

16 NACHO CHIPS

½ CUP PICO DE GALLO
(PAGE 34)

½ CUP HABANERO MAYO
(PAGE 71)

MAKES 16 NACHOS

IN A SMALL SKILLET, pour in canola oil to a depth of 1 inch and heat to 375 degrees F. Put the buttermilk and flour into 2 shallow bowls. Coat the oysters with the buttermilk, then dip them in the flour. When the oil is hot, slip in the oysters, a few at a time, and fry for 45 seconds to 1 minute, or until lightly browned. Transfer the oysters to paper towels to drain. Keep warm until all are cooked.

To serve, put a heaping teaspoonful of Pico de Gallo on each chip, and then a fried oyster. Top each with a heaping teaspoonful of Habanero Mayo. Serve immediately.

Serrano Ham Quesadillas

A QUESADILLA IS A GRILLED CHEESE SANDWICH MADE WITH TORTILLAS. LIKE ANY GRILLED CHEESE SANDWICH, A QUESADILLA TASTES EVEN BETTER WITH A LITTLE SOMETHING EXTRA INSIDE. OUR FAVORITES ARE MADE WITH SERRANO HAM (OR ANY OTHER FINE AIR-CURED HAM LIKE PROSCIUTTO, WESTPHALIAN, OR BAYONNE) AND OAXACAN STRING CHEESE.

DIVIDE THE HAM, cheese, and serrano chile evenly among 8 flour tortillas. Fold the tortillas in half.

In a medium-sized skillet, melt the butter over medium heat. (Plan on using $1/2$ teaspoon butter for each quesadilla in the pan.) When it starts to bubble, add as many of the folded tortillas as will fit easily in the pan. Toast for about 2 minutes on each side, or until the cheese melts and the tortilla is crisp. Serve the quesadillas piping hot.

Variation: These little folded-over ham quesadillas taste great right out of the skillet. But if you want to dress them up for company, make them with 2 tortillas each (sandwich style), then slice them into quarters and top with Nuevo Guacamole (page 78) and Picante Sauce (page 29).

8 OUNCES SERRANO HAM, PROSCIUTTO, OR OTHER GOOD HAM
THINLY SLICED

8 OUNCES PULLED OAXACAN STRING CHEESE OR GRATED JACK CHEESE

2 TABLESPOONS MINCED SERRANO CHILE, OR TO TASTE

SALT

8 FLOUR TORTILLAS

4 TEASPOONS BUTTER

MAKES 8 QUESADILLAS

Shown with Nuevo Guacamole (page 78) and Pico de Gallo (page 34).

Nopalito Quesadillas

THE PADS OF THE PRICKLY PEAR CACTUS, CALLED *NOPALITOS*, ARE A POPULAR VEGETABLE ON BOTH SIDES OF THE BORDER. WHEN CUT UP, THEY LOOK LIKE GREEN BEANS BUT HAVE A TART FLAVOR.

2 TABLESPOONS OLIVE OIL

10 OUNCES DICED PEELED CACTUS PADDLES

1/2 SMALL ONION
DICED

8 OUNCES PULLED OAXACAN
STRING CHEESE OR GRATED
MOZZARELLA CHEESE

2 TEASPOONS UNSALTED BUTTER

1 TABLESPOON DRIED MEXICAN OREGANO
OR MINCED FRESH MARJORAM

8 FLOUR TORTILLAS

BLACK BEAN RELISH
(PAGE 121)

MAKES 4 QUESADILLAS

IN A MEDIUM-SIZED SKILLET, heat the olive oil over high heat. Add the cactus and cook, stirring continuously, for 8 to 12 minutes, or until the cactus changes color and the slime disappears completely. Add the onion and cook, stirring, for 2 minutes, or until translucent. Remove from the heat and divide the cactus mixture among 4 tortillas. Sprinkle the cheese over the cactus (allow about 1/2 cup for each), and cover each tortilla with a second tortilla (like making a sandwich).

In a large skillet, melt 1/2 teaspoon of the butter over medium heat. When it starts to bubble, place a quesadilla in the skillet. Cook for 1 to 2 minutes on each side, or until the cheese has melted and the tortilla is crisp. Repeat with the remaining butter and quesadillas.

Place each quesadilla on a plate, and cut into quarters. Garnish with the Black Bean Relish.

Nopalito-Crab Quesadillas: Add 4 ounces fresh-cooked crabmeat, picked over for shells and flaked, with the onion.

Habanero Mayo

THIS IS AN OUTRAGEOUSLY TASTY TOPPING FOR ALL KINDS OF APPETIZERS, TACOS, AND SANDWICHES. IF YOU WANT TO CHEAT, YOU CAN MIX THE MUSTARD, HONEY, CILANTRO, AND MINCED CHILE INTO A CUP OF BOTTLED MAYONNAISE, BUT IT TASTES MUCH BETTER HOMEMADE.

IN A BLENDER, combine the mustard, honey, cilantro, habanero, egg yolks, lemon, and salt. Turn the blender on and off briefly to mix. Remove the inner part of the blender lid, if possible, or, failing that, remove the lid. With the blender running, gradually pour in the olive oil in a thin, steady stream, processing until the mixture thickens to a mayonnaise. Transfer to a bowl, cover, and refrigerate for up to 2 days.

2 TABLESPOONS DIJON MUSTARD

2 TABLESPOONS HONEY

1/2 CUP CHOPPED FRESH CILANTRO

1 TEASPOON MINCED HABANERO CHILE

2 EGG YOLKS

1 TABLESPOON FRESH LEMON JUICE

1/2 TEASPOON SEA SALT

3/4 CUP OLIVE OIL

MAKES 1 1/2 CUPS

Crab-Stuffed Anaheims

SEAFOOD-STUFFED CHILES ARE COMMON IN COASTAL MEXICO. THESE CRAB-FILLED ANAHEIMS ARE A LITTLE MORE DELICATE THAN THE TRADITIONAL POBLANO AND SHRIMP VERSION. THEY MAKE A ZESTY APPETIZER WITH A SIDE OF GUACAMOLE.

2 TABLESPOONS OLIVE OIL

2 SHALLOTS
DICED

1/2 CUP FRESH CORN KERNELS

1 CELERY STALK
FINELY DICED

18 OUNCES FRESH-COOKED CRABMEAT
PICKED OVER FOR SHELLS
AND FLAKED

1/2 CUP CRUMBLED FRESH GOAT CHEESE

**1 TABLESPOON CHOPPED
FRESH EPAZOTE (OPTIONAL)**

SALT

6 ANAHEIM PEPPERS
ROASTED AND PEELED
(SEE PAGE 142)

1 CUP NUEVO GUACAMOLE
(PAGE 78)

MAKES **6** STUFFED PEPPERS

PREHEAT AN OVEN TO 375 DEGREES F. In a medium-sized skillet, heat the olive oil over high heat. Add the shallots, corn, and celery and sauté for 3 minutes, or until the vegetables are wilted. Add the crabmeat and cook for 1 minute longer, or until just warm. Transfer the mixture to a small bowl. Fold the goat cheese into the crab mixture. Add the epazote, if using, and season to taste with salt.

Slit each pepper along one side and carefully remove the seeds, leaving the stem intact. Spoon an equal amount of the crab mixture into each pepper. Place slit-side up on a greased baking sheet. Place the stuffed peppers in the oven for 4 to 6 minutes, or until piping hot.

To serve, garnish each chile with the guacamole.

Stuffed Squash Blossoms: If you should find fresh squash blossoms in the market, you can use this same recipe to stuff 8 to 10 of them. Dip the stuffed blossoms in buttermilk, dredge them in all-purpose flour, and then fry them lightly in vegetable oil before you put them in the oven.

Shown with Nuevo Guacamole (page 78).

Pork and Raisin Pasillas

FRUITY PICADILLO-FILLED DRIED PEPPERS ARE A FAVORITE APPETIZER IN OAXACA. THE RECIPE IS EVEN BETTER WITH LEFTOVER COOKED PORK. JUST CHOP THE PORK VERY FINE AND ADD IT TO THE ONIONS AND GARLIC AFTER THEY ARE TRANSLUCENT.

8 PASILLA CHILES

2 TABLESPOONS OLIVE OIL

1 POUND GROUND PORK

3 CLOVES GARLIC
MINCED

1/2 ONION
FINELY DICED

1 CUP RAISINS
CHOPPED

1 TABLESPOON TARAMIND PASTE
(OPTIONAL)

1 TEASPOON GROUND CINNAMON

FRESHLY GROUND BLACK PEPPER

1/2 CUP TOMATO PUREE

1/4 CUP SLIVERED ALMONDS
TOASTED

SALT

SOUR CREAM

MAKES 6 STUFFED PEPPERS

PREHEAT AN OVEN TO 300 DEGREES. Place the pasilla chiles in a bowl and add hot water to cover. Let stand for 20 minutes, or until softened but not falling apart. In a medium-sized skillet, heat the oil over high heat. Add the pork, garlic, and onion and cook, stirring occasionally, for 8 to 12 minutes, or until the pork is nicely brown. Drain off any excess fat. Add the raisins, tamarind, cinnamon, black pepper, and tomato puree and cook for 3 to 4 minutes, or until the mixture bubbles. Add the almonds, season to taste with salt, and remove from the heat.

Drain the chiles and slit each pepper along one side. Carefully remove the seeds, leaving the stem intact. Spoon an equal amount of the pork mixture into each pepper. Place slit-side up on a greased baking sheet. Place the stuffed peppers in the oven for 3 to 4 minutes, or until piping hot.

Garnish with sour cream before serving.

Jalapeño Corn Slaw

YOU DON'T FIND MUCH COLESLAW IN MEXICO, BUT CABBAGE MARINATED WITH VINEGAR AND CHILES IS A POPULAR RELISH IN CENTRAL AMERICA. THIS RECIPE COMBINES THE CENTRAL AMERICAN CHILE-CABBAGE CONCEPT WITH GOOD OLD AMERICAN COLESLAW.

COMBINE ALL THE INGREDIENTS in a bowl, including salt to taste. Toss well. Cover and let stand in the refrigerator for 2 hours before serving. Serves 6-8 people.

½ HEAD GREEN CABBAGE
THINLY SLICED

2 CUPS ROASTED CORN KERNELS
(SEE PAGE 144)

2 RED BELL PEPPERS
ROASTED, PEELED, STEMMED, SEEDED, AND DICED (SEE PAGE 143)

1 RED ONION
DICED

3 TABLESPOONS FRESH LEMON JUICE

3 TABLESPOONS CHAMPAGNE VINEGAR

2 JALAPEÑO CHILES
STEMMED AND MINCED

1 CUP COARSELY CHOPPED FRESH CILANTRO

FRESHLY GROUND BLACK PEPPER

SALT

MAKES **4~5** CUPS

Shrimp Cocktail Huatulco

THESE MARTINI GLASSES FULL OF MANGO-AND-CHILE "COCKTAIL SAUCE" WITH GRILLED SHRIMP HANGING OVER THE RIM ARE SO BEAUTIFUL IT'S HARD TO GET YOUR GUESTS TO STOP STARING AND EAT THEM. BUT ONCE THEY TAKE A BITE, THEY'LL ASK FOR A SPOON TO CLEAN UP THE BOTTOM OF THE GLASS. WE NAMED OUR LOVELY SHRIMP COCKTAILS AFTER HUATULCO, OAXACA'S IMPOSSIBLY BEAUTIFUL SEASIDE RESORT.

HEAT THE GRILL. Season the shrimp with salt and pepper. Quickly grill the shrimp over a fairly hot fire, turning once, for about 2 minutes on each side, or until just done. Transfer to a dish, let cool, cover, and refrigerate until ready to eat.

In a bowl, combine the tomatillos, onion, ancho chile, lime juice, mango puree or nectar, cilantro, and tomato. Toss well and season to taste with salt. Let stand for 2 hours in the refrigerator.

Divide the mango mixture among 4 small martini glasses. Partially submerge 4 shrimp, heads first, in each glass, with the tails over the rim. Serve at once.

16 LARGE SHRIMP
PEELED AND DEVEINED
WITH TAIL FIN SEGMENT INTACT

SALT AND FRESHLY GROUND BLACK PEPPER

6 SMALL TOMATILLOS
HUSKED AND FINELY DICED

¼ ONION
MINCED

1 ANCHO CHILE
STEMMED, SEEDED, AND CUT
INTO FINE THREADS

2 TABLESPOONS FRESH LIME JUICE

1 CUP PUREED MANGO OR MANGO NECTAR

**¼ CUP FINELY CHOPPED
FRESH CILANTRO**

1 CUP DICED TOMATO

SERVES **4** PEOPLE

Nuevo Guacamole

HERE'S OUR RECIPE FOR GUACAMOLE. WE THINK THAT THE NONTRADITIONAL STEP OF COOKING THE ONIONS AND THE CHILES FIRST GIVES THEM A FULLER, ROASTED FLAVOR THAT GOES BEAUTIFULLY WITH THE MELLOW AVOCADO. JUST BE CAREFUL NOT TO STAND TOO CLOSE TO THE PAN WHILE COOKING THE CHILES. THE FUMES WILL BURN YOUR NOSE.

2 TEASPOONS UNSALTED BUTTER

2 TEASPOONS VEGETABLE OIL

3 SERRANO CHILES
STEMMED AND CUT IN HALF
LENGTHWISE

1 ONION
DICED

1¹/₂ TABLESPOONS FRESH LEMON JUICE

SALT

3 RIPE AVOCADOS
PITTED AND PEELED

¹/₂ CUP CHOPPED FRESH CILANTRO
(OPTIONAL)

MAKES **2** CUPS

IN A MEDIUM-SIZED SKILLET, melt the butter with the vegetable oil over high heat. Add the serrano chiles and onion and sauté for 3 to 5 minutes, or until lightly browned. Add the lemon juice, season to taste with salt, and remove from the heat.

Carefully transfer the chiles to a cutting board and chop finely. (Rubber gloves are a good idea.) Transfer the serrano mixture to a mixing bowl (or a *molcajete* if you have one). Add the avocados and mash until well mixed. Season to taste with salt. Serve immediately as a salad, a dip for tortilla chips, or a garnish.

Note: There are a lot of tips for keeping guacamole fresh. Some cooks say adding lots of lemon or lime juice helps. Some say that leaving the avocado pits in the guacamole keeps it from turning brown. We have never had any luck with either of these methods. The only way we know of to keep guacamole fresh is not to make more of it than you can eat right away.

The Whole Enchilada Family

NEw WAyS TO STuFF a TORTiLLa

CHAPTER

6

ONE AFTERNOON IN OAXACA, WE HAD AN ENCHILADA EPIPHANY. WE WERE EATING LUNCH IN A LITTLE RESTAURANT, AND AS WE surveyed the menu, we noticed three kinds of stuffed tortillas: enchiladas, *entomatadas*, and *enfrijoladas*. In an instant, the whole strange history of the word *enchilada* flashed before our eyes and we realized what the menu was trying to say. ♦ Despite its usage as a noun on both sides of the border, enchilada is actually an adjective in Spanish. The full name of the dish is *tortillas enchiladas*, or "chilied tortillas," and it refers to the original method of preparation, which called for the tortillas to be dipped in chile sauce and lightly fried. *Tortillas enchiladas* were called enchiladas for short. ♦ That definition seems clear enough. But it's not that simple. On the street in Mexico, an enchilada means a chile-dipped tortilla, but in a Mexican restaurant or coffee shop, it sometimes means a chile-dipped tortilla with a stuffing. And it can also be a tortilla that is dipped in something else entirely.

Entomatadas and *enfrijoladas* are tortillas dipped in tomato sauce and bean sauce, respectively. As we considered these words, it suddenly dawned on us that our favorite Tex-Mex entrée, *enchiladas verdes*, wouldn't be considered enchiladas at all in this restaurant. The tomatillo sauce would actually make them *entomatadas verdes*.

Of course, these words aren't widely used outside of Oaxaca. A stuffed tortilla in a *tomatillo* sauce is still called an enchilada in other parts of Mexico. But the menu in that little Oaxacan restaurant got us thinking about all the different things we call enchiladas—the stacked enchiladas of New Mexico, the rolled enchiladas of Mexican and Texan coffee shop fame, the chilied tortillas on the street in Mexican cities, and all the versions that don't even use a chile sauce. While we where sitting there looking at the menu,

we couldn't resist ordering the *enfrijoladas*, a version of stuffed tortillas we had never seen in Texas.

The dish that was delivered to our table was a humble masterpiece. The creamy black bean sauce with the soft, cheese-filled tortillas had the same satisfying effect on us as a large pile of mashed potatoes and gravy. Ever since then, we have thought of *enfrijoladas* as Mexican comfort food.

We've borrowed the Oaxacan definitions for the stuffed tortillas in this chapter. And we've included lots of recipes for the enchilada's tasty cousins, the *entomatada* and the *enfrijolada*. As you'll see, bean sauces and tomato sauces give the stuffed tortilla a wider range of flavors. They are milder, too, which makes them a good balance for other spicier dishes.

Beef and Potato Enchiladas

HERE'S AN OLD-FASHIONED ENCHILADA, THE KIND THAT GAVE THE DISH ITS NAME.

2 LARGE BAKING POTATOES

5 ANCHO CHILES
STEMMED AND SEEDED

3 GUAJILLO CHILES
STEMMED AND SEEDED

1 RED ONION
THINLY SLICED

1 TABLESPOON FRESH LEMON JUICE

SALT

½ CUP ROASTED GARLIC PUREE
(SEE PAGE 145)

1 TABLESPOON ACHIOTE PASTE
(SEE PAGE 142)

2 TABLESPOONS PLUS ½ CUP OLIVE OIL

1 POUND BEEF TENDERLOIN
CUT INTO BITE-SIZED CHUNKS

FRESHLY GROUND PEPPER

2 CUPS CHOPPED SPINACH

8 CORN TORTILLAS

1 CUP CRUMBLED FETA CHEESE

½ CUP CHOPPED FRESH CILANTRO

MAKES 8 ENCHILADAS

BAKE THE POTATOES in a 350-degree oven for 50 minutes.

Meanwhile, soak the chiles in hot water for 30 minutes. Marinate half of the onion with the lemon juice and salt. Drain the chiles, reserving the water, and transfer them to a blender. Add the garlic puree, achiote paste, and 1 cup of the chile water. Blend until smooth. Transfer to a shallow bowl and season to taste with salt. Set aside.

In a medium skillet, heat the 2 tablespoons oil over high heat. Add the beef and the unmarinated onion and cook, stirring, for 2 minutes, or until the beef is seared. Add the spinach and cook and stir for 1 minute, or until wilted. Remove from the heat.

When the potatoes are cool enough to handle, peel and mash them lightly. Add the beef mixture to the potatoes along with salt and pepper to taste. Mix well.

Place the same skillet over a medium heat and add the ½ cup oil. Once hot, dip each tortilla into it for 2 seconds, then into the chile mixture until well coated, and finally back into the oil. Cook each for 10 to 20 seconds, or until the tortilla is soft, and drain on paper towels.

Divide the beef mixture among the tortillas, roll them up, and place them seam-side down in a greased baking dish. Top them with the chile sauce. Place in the oven for 7 minutes, or until bubbling hot.

Remove from the oven, transfer to plates, and garnish with the onion, feta, and cilantro.

Chicken Mole Enchiladas

IN OAXACA, THESE GO BY THE NAME *ENMOLADAS*. THE COMBINATION OF CHICKEN AND MOLE SAUCE HAS BEEN POPULAR IN TEX-MEX RESTAURANTS FOR MANY YEARS. SERVE THESE WITH MEXICAN MARIGOLD MINT RICE (PAGE 122).

PREHEAT AN OVEN TO 300 DEGREES F. In a medium-sized skillet, heat 2 tablespoons of the olive oil over medium heat. Add the chicken and onion, and cook, stirring, for 4 to 5 minutes, or until the chicken is cooked through. Remove from the heat and place in a bowl with 1/2 cup of the mole sauce. Toss well and set aside.

Wipe out the skillet and add the remaining 4 tablespoons olive oil. Place over medium heat. When the oil is hot, dip a tortilla into the hot oil and cook for 10 to 15 seconds on each side, or until soft. Drain on paper towels. Repeat with the remaining tortillas.

Divide the chicken mixture evenly among the tortillas, roll them up, and place them seam-side down in a greased baking dish. Pour the remaining 1 1/2 cups mole sauce over them. Arrange the cheese slices evenly on top. Place in the oven for 12 to 15 minutes, or until bubbling hot.

Remove from the oven, transfer to plates, and garnish with the sesame seeds.

6 TABLESPOONS OLIVE OIL

2 WHOLE CHICKEN BREASTS, 10 OUNCES EACH
SKINNED, BONED, AND JULIENNED

1/4 CUP DICED ONION

2 CUPS MOLE TEJANO
(PAGE 94)

1/4 CUP OLIVE OIL

8 CORN TORTILLAS

4 SLICES *QUESO BLANCO*, JACK, OR MOZZARELLA CHEESE

1/4 CUP SESAME SEEDS
TOASTED

MAKES 8 ENCHILADAS

Chipotle Shrimp Entomatadas

THINK OF THAT ITALIAN CLASSIC, PASTA WITH SHRIMP AND TOMATO SAUCE. NOW SUBSTITUTE A TORTILLA FOR THE PASTA AND YELLOW *ENTOMATADA* SAUCE FOR THE MARINARA. THE GARLIC AND THE PEPPERS ARE ALREADY THERE.

PREHEAT AN OVEN TO 300 DEGREES F. In a skillet, heat 1 tablespoon of the oil over high heat. Add the shrimp and onion and cook, stirring, for 2 minutes. Add the garlic puree, parsley, tomatoes, and chipotle puree. Season to taste with salt. Transfer to a bowl and set aside.

Wipe out the skillet and add the remaining 1/4 cup olive oil. Place over medium heat. When the oil is hot, dip a tortilla into the hot oil and cook for 10 to 15 seconds on each side, or until soft. Drain on paper towels. Repeat with the remaining tortillas.

Divide the shrimp stuffing evenly among the tortillas, roll them up, and place them seam-side down in a greased baking dish. Pour the habanero sauce over the top. Place in the oven for 10 minutes, or until bubbling hot.

Remove from the oven, transfer to plates, and garnish with the cilantro sprigs. Serve at once.

5 TABLESPOONS OLIVE OIL

16 MEDIUM-SIZED SHRIMP
PEELED, DEVEINED, AND CUT INTO CHUNKS

1 ONION
DICED

1/4 CUP ROASTED GARLIC PUREE
(SEE PAGE 145)

1/2 CUP MINCED FRESH PARSLEY

2 CUPS DICED TOMATOES

2 TABLESPOONS CHIPOTLE PUREE
(SEE PAGE 144)

SALT

8 CORN TORTILLAS

YELLOW TOMATO–HABANERO SAUCE
(PAGE 91)

4 FRESH CILANTRO SPRIGS

MAKES 8 ENCHILADAS

Shown with Yellow Tomato Habanero Sauce (page 91).

Wild Mushroom Mole Enchiladas

SERVE THESE HEARTY VEGETARIAN ENCHILADAS WITH WHITE
BEAN REFRITO (PAGE 119) AND RICE FOR A SATISFYING
MEAL OR AS A SIDE DISH WITH GRILLED MEATS.

1/2 CUP OLIVE OIL

1 POUND ASSORTED MUSHROOMS,
SUCH AS CHANTERELLES, SHIITAKES,
OYSTERS, AND PORTOBELLOS
SLICED

1 CUP CHOPPED SCALLIONS

2 TABLESPOONS MINCED FRESH
EPAZOTE OR MARJORAM

1/4 CUP MINCED FRESH CILANTRO

1 CUP CRUMBLED FRESH GOAT CHEESE

3 TABLESPOONS ROASTED GARLIC PUREE
(SEE PAGE 145)

8 CORN TORTILLAS

2 CUPS MOLE TEJANO
(PAGE 94)

1/4 CUP SESAME SEEDS
TOASTED

MAKES 8 ENCHILADAS

PREHEAT AN OVEN TO 350 DEGREES F. In a
medium-sized skillet, heat 1/4 cup of the olive oil
over medium heat. Add the mushrooms and sauté for 3
to 5 minutes, or until the mushrooms start to wilt. Add
the scallions, epazote, and cilantro and sauté for 2 minutes, or until the mushrooms are tender. Transfer to a
bowl and add the goat cheese and garlic puree. Mix
well and set aside.

Wipe out the skillet and add the remaining 1/4
cup olive oil. Place over medium heat. When the oil is
hot, dip a tortilla in the hot oil and cook for 10 to 15
seconds on each side, or until soft. Drain on paper
towels. Repeat with the remaining tortillas.

Divide the mushroom stuffing evenly among the
tortillas, roll them up, and place seam-side down in a
greased baking dish. Pour the mole over the top.
Place in the oven for 10 minutes, or until bubbling hot.

Remove from the oven, transfer to plates, and
garnish with the sesame seeds.

Duck Enfrijoladas Blancas

THE CRISPY DUCK *CHICHARRÓNES* ARE A DELIGHTFUL SURPRISE WITH THE TENDER DARK DUCK MEAT AND SMOOTH WHITE BEAN SAUCE. SAVE THE DUCK BREASTS FOR DUCK BREAST IN GREEN MOLE (PAGE 98).

PLACE A MEDIUM SAUCEPAN over medium heat and sear the duck pieces skin-side down for 2 to 4 minutes. Turn the pieces and sear on the second side for 2 to 4 minutes, or until light brown. Add the bay leaf, onion, pasilla chiles, lemon juice, beer, water, and cinnamon. Bring to a boil, immediately reduce the heat to low, and simmer, uncovered, for $2^1/_2$ hours, or until the duck is tender. Add water as needed to keep the duck covered.

Preheat an oven to 300 degrees F. Remove the duck from the saucepan and, when cool enough to handle, cut the skin away on each leg and thigh, removing it in a single piece. Pull the meat off the bone and set it aside. Place the duck skins in a baking pan in the oven and cook for 10 to 15 minutes, or until very crisp. Chop into small pieces and set it aside.

In a medium-sized skillet, heat the oil over medium heat. When hot, dip the tortilla into the hot oil and cook for 10 to 15 seconds on each side, or until soft. Drain on paper towels. Repeat with the remaining tortillas.

Divide the meat and skin evenly among the tortillas. Roll them up and place them seam-side down in a greased baking dish. Cover with the bean sauce and sprinkle with the Jack cheese. Place in the oven for 6 to 10 minutes, or until hot in the middle.

Serve garnished with the Pineapple Pico.

4 DUCK LEGS WITH THIGHS

1 BAY LEAF

$^1/_2$ ONION
QUARTERED

2 PASILLA CHILES
STEMMED AND SEEDED

1 TABLESPOON FRESH LEMON JUICE

ONE BOTTLE (12 OUNCES) BEER

$1^1/_2$ CUPS WATER

PINCH OF GROUND CINNAMON

$^1/_4$ CUP OLIVE OIL

8 CORN TORTILLAS

WHITE BEAN SAUCE
(PAGE 90)

1 CUP GRATED JACK CHEESE

1 CUP PINEAPPLE PICO
(PAGE 35)

M A K E S **8** ENFRIJOLADAS

Goat Cheese Enfrijoladas Negras

HERE IS AN INSPIRED CONTEMPORARY VERSION OF THAT FAMOUS TEX-MEX COMBINATION OF BEANS AND CHEESE. IF YOU THOUGHT YOU LIKED REFRIED BEANS AND CHEDDAR, WAIT UNTIL YOU TASTE THESE TORTILLAS STUFFED WITH GOAT CHEESE TOPPED WITH BLACK BEAN SAUCE. SERVE WITH VANILLA RICE (PAGE 123).

12 OUNCES FRESH GOAT CHEESE
AT ROOM TEMPERATURE

1 TABLESPOON CHOPPED FRESH EPAZOTE OR CILANTRO OR 2 TEASPOONS DRIED EPAZOTE

4 SCALLIONS
CHOPPED

SALT

1/4 CUP VEGETABLE OIL

8 CORN TORTILLAS

BLACK BEAN SAUCE
HEATED (SEE NEXT PAGE)

1 CUP PINEAPPLE PICO
(PAGE 35)

4 FRESH CILANTRO SPRIGS

MAKES 8 ENFRIJOLADAS

PREHEAT AN OVEN TO 325 DEGREES F. In a small bowl, combine the goat cheese, epazote or cilantro, and scallions. Stir well, season with salt, and set aside.

In a medium-sized skillet, heat the vegetable oil over medium heat. When the oil is hot, dip a tortilla into the hot oil and cook for 10 to 15 seconds on each side, or until soft. Drain on paper towels. Repeat with the remaining tortillas.

Divide the goat cheese mixture evenly among the tortillas, roll them up, and place seam-side down in a greased baking pan. Place in the oven and bake for 5 minutes, or until the cheese melts.

Remove from the oven and transfer to plates. Cover with the bean sauce. Garnish with the Pineapple Pico and cilantro sprigs.

White Bean Sauce

SUBSTITUTE BEAN SAUCE FOR THE CHILE SAUCE IN ANY ENCHILADA RECIPE TO TURN "CHILIED" TORTILLAS INTO "BEANED" TORTILLAS. FOR AN ELEGANT LOOK, MAKE "TWO-TONE" ENFRIJOLADAS. POUR WHITE BEAN SAUCE ON ONE HALF OF THE STUFFED TORTILLAS AND BLACK BEAN SAUCE ON THE OTHER.

2 TABLESPOONS OLIVE OIL

¼ ONION
FINELY DICED

1 CLOVE GARLIC
MINCED

½ TEASPOON GROUND CUMIN

½ TEASPOON PAPRIKA

½ TEASPOON GUAJILLO CHILE POWDER
(SEE PAGE 144)

1½ CUPS COOKED
WHITE BEANS WITH BROTH
(SEE PAGE 116)

½ CUP SOUR CREAM

SALT

MAKES ABOUT 2 CUPS

IN A LARGE SKILLET, heat the olive oil over medium heat. Add the onion and garlic and sauté for 3 to 4 minutes, or until translucent. Add the cumin, paprika, and guajillo chile powder and sauté for 1 minute. Add the beans and sour cream and bring to a boil. Reduce the heat to low and simmer for 3 minutes.

Transfer 1 cup of the bean mixture to a blender and puree until smooth. To remove the bean skins, pass the puree through a sieve back into the skillet, then simmer for 2 minutes until heated through. If the sauce becomes too thick, thin with water. Season to taste with salt. Use warm, or cover and store in refrigerator; it will keep for up to 4 days.

Black Bean Sauce: Substitute cooked black beans and proceed as directed.

Yellow Tomato-Habanero Sauce

WHEN YOU USE TOMATO SAUCE INSTEAD OF CHILE SAUCE, YOU'RE MAKING ENTOMATADAS. TO MAKE "TWO-TONE" ENTOMATADAS, POUR WARM GREEN SAUCE (PAGE 31) ON ONE HALF OF THE STUFFED TORTILLAS AND THIS SAUCE ON THE OTHER.

IN A FOOD PROCESSOR, combine the garlic, habanero chile, onion, tomatoes, oregano, and lemon juice. Puree until smooth. Season with salt. Strain through a fine-mesh sieve into a bowl and let stand for 3 hours so the lemon and salt have time to mellow the flavors of the garlic and onion.

In a medium-sized saucepan, heat the olive oil over medium heat. Slowly add the puree, being careful the oil doesn't splash. Cook, stirring occasionally, for 2 to 5 minutes, or until the sauce thickens. This will keep for up to 4 days in the refrigerator.

2 CLOVES GARLIC
HALVED

$1/4$ HABANERO CHILE
SEEDED

$1/2$ ONION
DICED

2 LARGE YELLOW TOMATOES
HALVED AND SEEDED

1 TEASPOON MINCED FRESH OREGANO, PREFERABLY MEXICAN

2 TABLESPOONS FRESH LEMON JUICE

SALT

1 TABLESPOON OLIVE OIL

4 FRESH DILL SPRIGS

MAKES ABOUT **2** CUPS

CHAPTER 7

The Mystique of Mole

HOLy MOLeS aND IRReVEReNT MOLES

WHEN THE WORD *MOLE* IS MENTIONED, MOST PEOPLE THINK OF *MOLE POBLANO*, THE MOLE WITH THE CHOCOLATE IN IT. AND SINCE MOLE poblano is a pretty strange sauce, many people have therefore dismissed the entire subject of mole. We can sympathize. Although we have made our pilgrimage to the famed convent kitchen in Puebla where the nun of legend cooked up the sauce, we have never had a lot of faith in the whole business. ▼ The legend is pretty dubious, but it seems to have given some sort of religious significance to the very complicated recipe. Authentic *mole poblano* recipes call for up to twenty ingredients and require all sorts of toasting, frying, and mashing steps. The result is a complicated sauce that you don't want to eat every day. One Mexican author says that to appreciate *mole poblano*, you have to share the Mexican love for the baroque.

But *mole poblano* is not the only mole in Mexico. You can find dozens of different mole pastes for sale in Mexican markets. There are moles made with nuts, moles made with fruits, and moles made with herbs. After all, mole comes from the Nahuatl word *molli*, and all it really means is "mashed up." A traditional mole is made in a *molcajete* (the Mexican mortar), which comes from the same Nahuatl word. Once upon a time, moles were made by mashing up whatever ingredients were on hand. If you think about it, that avocado dip you love so much is a mole, too.

These Nuevo Tex-Mex moles were conceived in the original spirit of mashing up something on the spur of the moment that goes well with what you're cooking. Pork Chops in Apple Butter Mole probably bears little resemblance to anything you've ever called mole before, but once you've tasted it, we hope you'll join us in asking, "Why not?"

We have also departed from the tradition of always using mole as a braising sauce. When chicken is served with mole in Mexican and Tex-Mex restaurants, it is always simmered in the sauce. But that means every time you serve mole, you have to eat stewed meat. No wonder people get tired of it. Long-cooked meats are fine, but juicy grilled meats are much more popular these days. So we have adapted some of our moles to the way we actually cook.

For those who do love traditional *mole poblano*, we've also provided a couple of recipes based on that "holy mole." Because baroque is nice, too, every once in a while.

Mole Tejano

GATHERING AND PREPARING THE TWELVE TO TWENTY-FOUR INGRE-
DIENTS FOR CLASSIC *MOLE POBLANO* CAN TAKE HOURS AND HOURS,
AND WE'VE ALWAYS WONDERED WHETHER SOME OF THE MORE
TEDIOUS STEPS, LIKE SCORCHING THE TORTILLAS AND TOASTING
THE CHILE SEEDS, WERE ADDING ALL THAT MUCH TO THE SAUCE.
SO WE DEVISED THIS EASY BUT DELICIOUS MOLE OF OUR OWN. IT
MAY NOT BE AS COMPLEX AS HOMEMADE *MOLE POBLANO*, BUT IT
SURE TASTES BETTER THAN THE STUFF YOU BUY IN THE BOTTLE.

2 TABLESPOONS OLIVE OIL

2 CLOVES GARLIC
MINCED

1/4 ONION
SLICED

2 TOMATOES
PEELED AND QUARTERED

1 ANCHO CHILE
STEMMED AND SEEDED

1 PASILLA CHILE
STEMMED AND SEEDED

1 OUNCE SEMISWEET CHOCOLATE
BROKEN INTO PIECES

1/4 TEASPOON SESAME SEEDS

1/4 TEASPOON CHOPPED ALMONDS

1/2 TEASPOON SUGAR

1 CUP CHICKEN STOCK

SALT

MAKES ABOUT 2 CUPS

IN A MEDIUM-SIZED SAUCEPAN, heat the olive oil over medium heat. Add the garlic and onion and sauté for 5 minutes, or until translucent. Add the tomatoes, ancho chile, pasilla chile, chocolate, sesame seeds, almonds, sugar, and chicken stock. Simmer for 5 minutes.

Transfer the mixture to a blender and puree until smooth. Season to taste with salt. Pour into a bowl to check the texture. If the mole has any grittiness, return it to the blender and puree again. Use warm, or cover and store in the refrigerator for up to 1 week.

Chicken in Mole Tejano

HERE'S OUR VERSION OF TEX-MEX CHICKEN IN MOLE SAUCE. IT IS GREAT WITH ANNATTO RICE WITH WILD MUSHROOMS (PAGE 124) AND A BOWL OF CHARRO BEANS (PAGE 116).

PREHEAT AN OVEN TO 350 DEGREES F. In an ovenproof skillet, heat the olive oil over high heat. When the oil is hot, add the chicken breasts skin-side down and cook for about 5 minutes, or until the skin becomes crisp. Turn the chicken pieces and cook on the other side for 3 minutes, or until light brown. Transfer the chicken to a baking dish, skin-side down. Pour the mole evenly over the top.

Place in the oven for 5 to 7 minutes, or until the chicken is cooked through. Divide the chicken breasts among 4 plates. To garnish, sprinkle each plate with 1 teaspoon of the sesame seeds, and top each breast with 1 tablespoon of the sour cream.

2 TABLESPOONS OLIVE OIL

4 BONELESS CHICKEN BREAST HALVES

MOLE TEJANO
(PAGE 94)

4 TEASPOONS SESAME SEEDS
TOASTED

4 TABLESPOONS SOUR CREAM

SERVES 4 PEOPLE

Pork chops in Apple Butter Mole

APPLE BUTTER HAS ALWAYS BEEN A FAVORITE BREAKFAST SPREAD OF OURS, SO WE OFTEN HAVE SOME IN THE REFRIGERATOR. IT LENDS ITSELF BEAUTIFULLY TO THE MOLE TRADITION, IMPARTING AN AMAZING RICHNESS. SINCE THE PORK CHOPS AREN'T BRAISED IN THE MOLE, THEY CAN BE COOKED JUST THE WAY YOU LIKE THEM. SERVE WITH ANCHO CHILES STUFFED WITH SWEET POTATOES (PAGE 125).

HEAT THE GRILL. In a small bowl, combine the apple, lemon juice, and water. Set aside for the garnish. In a medium-sized skillet, heat the olive oil over medium heat. Add the onion and the guajillo and chipotle chiles and sauté for 2 to 4 minutes, or until the onion is translucent. Add the apple butter, cinnamon, and chicken stock. Bring to boil, stirring occasionally, and remove from the heat. Transfer to a blender and puree until smooth.

In the same skillet, melt the butter over medium heat until it bubbles. Pour the sauce from the blender into the hot butter and simmer for 2 minutes, stirring constantly to sear the sauce. Keep warm.

On the heated grill, cook the pork chops, turning a couple of times, for about 10 to 12 minutes, or to desired doneness.

Spoon a generous amount of the sauce onto each of 4 plates and put 1 grilled pork chop on each. Drain the apple pieces and place 2 apple wedges on each pork chop. Serve at once.

Shown with an Ancho Chile Stuffed with Sweet Potato (page 125) garnished with Chipotle Sour Cream (page 57), and a corn husk filled with Black Bean Relish (page 121).

1 APPLE
CORED AND SLICED INTO 8 WEDGES

1 TABLESPOON FRESH LEMON JUICE

1 CUP WATER

1 TABLESPOON OLIVE OIL

$\frac{1}{4}$ ONION
FINELY DICED

1 GUAJILLO CHILE
STEMMED AND SEEDED

1 CHIPOTLE CHILE
STEMMED AND SEEDED

1 CUP APPLE BUTTER

PINCH OF GROUND CINNAMON

1 CUP CHICKEN STOCK

1 TABLESPOON BUTTER

4 PORK CHOPS
8 OUNCES EACH

SERVES **4** PEOPLE

Duck Breast in Green Mole

DUCK AND GREEN MOLE IS A TRADITIONAL MEXICAN COMBINATION. BUT INSTEAD OF STEWING THE DUCK BREAST IN THE MOLE, WE GRILL IT MEDIUM-RARE AND SERVE IT LIKE A STEAK. SAVE THE DUCK LEGS AND THIGHS FOR DUCK ENFRIJOLADAS BLANCAS (PAGE 87).

1 TABLESPOON OLIVE OIL

1/2 ONION
JULIENNED

5 TOMATILLOS
HUSKED AND HALVED

1 CUP CHOPPED FRESH CILANTRO

3/4 CUP PINE NUTS
TOASTED

SALT

4 BONELESS DUCK BREAST HALVES

4 TABLESPOONS PAPAYA-HABANERO SALSA
(PAGE 30)

SERVES 4 PEOPLE

PREHEAT A BROILER. In a medium skillet, combine the oil, onion, and tomatillos over medium heat. Cook, stirring occasionally, for 4 to 7 minutes, or until the tomatillos are soft. Transfer to a blender and puree until smooth. Strain to remove the tomatillo skins and return the sieved mixture to the blender. Add the cilantro and 1/2 cup of the pine nuts and puree until smooth. Season to taste with salt and set aside in a warm spot.

Season the duck breasts with salt. Place a medium-sized skillet over high heat. Cook the duck breasts skin-side down for 5 to 8 minutes, or until the skin starts to brown. Turn the duck breasts over and cook for 1 minute longer. Transfer the duck breasts skin-side up to a broiler pan. Place the duck breasts in the broiler and broil for 5 minutes for medium-rare, or to desired doneness. The skin should be quite crisp.

While the duck breasts are cooking, drain the duck fat from the skillet used to cook the breasts. Measure 1 tablespoon of the duck fat and return it to the pan. Place over medium heat. When the duck fat is hot, slowly add the reserved mole, being careful it does not splash you. Bring to a slow boil, then remove from the heat; set aside in a warm spot.

Slice the duck breast thinly on the diagonal. Place a generous amount of sauce on each of 4 plates and fan the duck slices over the sauce. Garnish the sauce with the remaining 1/4 cup pine nuts, and put 1 tablespoon of salsa on top of each serving of duck.

Note: The step in which you add the mole to the hot pan is called "searing the sauce." It brightens the color and enhances the flavor.

Quail in Almond Mole

FOUR HALF QUAIL BREASTS MAKE A LOVELY DINNER WITH A SIDE DISH LIKE ANNATO RICE WITH WILD MUSHROOMS (PAGE 124). BUT THIS DISH MAKES AN EVEN MORE SPECTACULAR APPETIZER ON A LARGE, DECORATIVE PLATE.

HEAT THE GRILL. In a saucepan, heat 2 tablespoons of the olive oil over medium heat. Add the garlic and onion and cook, stirring occasionally, for 5 minutes, or until translucent. Add the tomatoes and guajillo and ancho chiles and cook, stirring, for 3 minutes. Add the stock, $1/2$ cup of the almonds, and the chocolate, sugar, cinnamon, and cloves. Cook for 3 to 5 minutes, or until the chiles start softening. Transfer to a blender and puree until smooth. Season to taste with salt. Set aside in a warm spot.

Arrange the quail halves over a hot fire and cook, turning once, for 3 to 4 minutes on each side, or to desired doneness. To serve as a main dish, place 4 quail halves on each plate and cover with the sauce. Garnish with the remaining $1/4$ cup almonds and the cilantro sprigs.

To serve as an appetizer: Spoon the mole into the dish, then place the quail halves in a circle, breast side in, so that the legs can be used as handles and the mole can be used as a dipping sauce. Pass the platter around and have a little bowl handy for the bones.

4 TABLESPOONS OLIVE OIL

2 CLOVES GARLIC
CHOPPED

$1/4$ ONION
DICED

2 TOMATOES
QUARTERED

1 GUAJILLO CHILE
STEMMED AND SEEDED

2 ANCHO CHILES
STEMMED AND SEEDED

1 CUP CHICKEN STOCK

$3/4$ CUP SLICED ALMONDS
TOASTED

2 TABLESPOONS CHOPPED
SEMISWEET CHOCOLATE

1 TABLESPOON SUGAR

$1/4$ TEASPOON GROUND CINNAMON

PINCH OF GROUND CLOVES

SALT

8 QUAILS
CUT IN HALF AND
BREAST BONES REMOVED

4 FRESH CILANTRO SPRIGS

SERVES 4 PEOPLE

Lamb chops in Banana-Mint Mole

THE UNCTUOUS TEXTURE AND TROPICAL FLAVOR OF COOKED BANANAS ADD A NEW DIMENSION TO THE FAMILIAR COMBINATION OF LAMB AND MINT. THIS IS ONE OF THE RICHEST MOLES YOU'LL EVER TASTE. SERVE WITH VANILLA RICE.

1 BANANA

10 FRESH MINT LEAVES

2 TABLESPOONS FRESH LEMON JUICE

3 TABLESPOONS OLIVE OIL

8 LAMB CHOPS
ABOUT 5 OUNCES EACH

SALT

1 CLOVE GARLIC
CHOPPED

1/2 ONION
SLICED

2 GUAJILLO CHILES
STEMMED AND SEEDED

4 DATES
PITTED

1 CUP CHICKEN STOCK

SERVES 4 PEOPLE

Shown with Vanilla Rice (page 123).

PREHEAT AN OVEN TO 400 DEGREES F. Peel the banana and cut it in half. Finely dice half of the banana and place in a small bowl. Mince 4 of the mint leaves and add to the bowl along with 1 tablespoon of the lemon juice. Toss well and set aside for the garnish. Coarsely chop the remaining banana half, and mince the remaining 6 mint leaves. Set aside.

In a skillet, heat 2 tablespoons of the olive oil over high heat. Season the lamb chops with salt and add to the skillet. Sear for 1 to 2 minutes on each side, or until lightly browned. Transfer the chops to a baking dish and place in the oven. Bake for 6 to 8 minutes for medium-rare, or to desired doneness.

Meanwhile, in the same skillet over medium heat, combine the remaining 1 tablespoon olive oil, the garlic, and the onion. Cook, stirring occasionally, for 3 minutes, or until the onion is translucent. Add the guajillo chiles, the coarsely chopped banana and minced mint, dates, the remaining 1 tablespoon lemon juice, and the chicken stock. Cook, stirring, for 4 to 6 minutes, or until the chiles are softened. Transfer to a blender and puree until smooth. Season with salt.

Place a generous amount of banana mole on each plate and place 2 lamb chops on each pool of sauce. Top each lamb chop with a spoonful of the banana-mint garnish and serve at once.

Fajita Feasts

GRILLED MEaTS aND A TABLeFUL OF TREaTS

CHAPTER 8

FAJITAS ARE A TEX-MEX PHENOMENON. ASK FOR FAJITAS IN MEXICO CITY AND YOU WILL PROBABLY BE DIRECTED TO THE NEAREST LINGERIE store. That's because in Spanish *faja* means "girdle" and *fajita* means "little girdle" or "little belt." Sounds strange? Well, consider that the word *fajita* actually describes the same piece of meat we call skirt steak in English. ☞ The skirt steak was one of the many lower grade beef cuts traditionally eaten by ranch hands in northern Mexico and Texas. When the ranch owners slaughtered a steer, the prime cuts would go to the ranch house and the rest of the animal would be divided among the help. Many old border dishes such as *barbacoa*, from the cow's head, and *menudo*, from the stomach lining, trace their beginnings to this custom.

With the advent of refrigeration and commercial slaughterhouses, the old ranch customs of meat distribution died out. Ranch hands and ranch owners bought their beef in the grocery store like everybody else. By the early 1960s, most Texas butchers threw the skirt steak cuts in with the other scraps they used for ground meat. But some butchers in the Lower Rio Grande Valley put the inner skirt aside for customers who still liked to grill the fajitas the way it was done in the old days. One of those traditionalists was Sonny Falcon.

Sonny Falcon, the man whom the *Laredo Times* called the Fajita King, set up a concession stand and sold his grilled fajita tacos for the first time at an outdoor festival in Kyle, Texas, in 1969. Falcon's tacos made fajitas famous, but they bore little resemblance to what we usually think of as fajitas. Falcon used only the thick meat of the inner skirt in his tacos. He never marinated the meat. It was simply trimmed, butterflied (cut in half lengthwise), grilled, and then chopped against the grain into bite-sized pieces.

Falcon's fajitas became a favorite at fairs and outdoor events all over Texas. But when people tried to cook Falcon's fajitas at home, they ended up buying the tough outer skirt because it had the same name and was less expensive. The marinades and tenderizing treatments that are associated with fajitas are a result of this confusion. But whether they were made with the tender inner skirt or the tenderized outer skirt, fajitas became such a fad that the price of fajita meat skyrocketed.

One of the first establishments to cash in on the fajita craze was the restaurant in Austin's Hyatt Hotel. But since fajita meat required so much preparation, they substituted sirloin. The Hyatt also began the practice of serving the sliced, grilled meat with a pile of soft flour tortillas and other taco fillings such as guacamole, sour cream, and salsa, so that patrons could roll their own tacos at the table.

The meaning of the Spanish word became fuzzy as more and more restaurants used the word *fajitas* to describe a tabletop buffet of grilled meats, soft tortillas, and condiments. As a result, any grilled food served with fillings and tortillas came to be called fajitas, including chicken fajitas, shrimp fajitas, fish fajitas, and even veggie fajitas.

For years, Sonny Falcon argued that fish fajitas and chicken fajitas, which might be translated as fish skirts and chicken girdles, were completely meaningless terms. But no one paid much attention to the finer points of Spanish translation. Eventually, Falcon gave up. In his short-lived restaurant in Austin, The Fajita King, he too started serving chicken fajitas. "It killed me to do it, but I got tired of trying to explain it to everybody," Falcon conceded.

If you think of fajitas as skirt steaks, we've got you covered. This chapter includes a recipe for Falcon's originals and for our own marinated version. And if you think of fajitas as a tableful of sizzling grilled meats, caramelized onions, freshly made salsas, countless condiments, and warm tortillas, we can take care of that, too.

Like Falcon, we've bowed to the popular notion of fajitas. The grilled meats and seafoods in this chapter are designed to be spread out on the table with condiments and tortillas. That way your family and friends can make their own tacos just the way they like them. So no matter what you are grilling — steak, shrimp, chicken, skirt steak — when they ask you what's for dinner, just say "fajitas." As Sonny Falcon would agree, it's easier than trying to explain the whole thing.

A Fajita Spread

The traditional condiments served with fajitas might include Nuevo Guacamole (page 78), Rajas (see page 143), Pico de Gallo (page 34), Picante Sauce (page 29), sour cream, grated cheese, shredded lettuce, chopped tomatoes, grilled onions, chopped cilantro, Refried Beans (page 119), pickled or fresh jalapeños, and lime quarters.

A few other Nuevo Tex-Mex recipes you might want to add to this list include some of the others salsas from Chapter 2, chipotle sour cream (see Chicken-Fried Tuna Tacos, page 57), and Black Bean Relish (page 121).

Grilling

Grilling means cooking close to the coals at high heat for a short time. Steaks, fish fillets, shrimp, and other quick-cooking foods do well with this high-heat method. The flavor of the fire is imparted to the outside of the food while sealing the moisture inside. Strongly flavored woods such as mesquite are great for grilling, since the food spends only a short time on the fire.

Here are a few grilled meats and seafoods to include in a fajita spread. Don't feel limited to making just one recipe. As long as you've got the grill going, you may as well make your feast a mixed grill.

Sonny Falcon's Original Fajitas

HERE'S SONNY'S RECIPE, AS EXPLAINED BY HIS SON DANNY. SONNY USUALLY SERVES HIS FAJITA TACOS WITH A LITTLE SALSA PICANTE AND A WHOLE LOT OF MEAT.

---

1 POUND FAJITA FLAP MEAT

SALT AND FRESHLY
GROUND BLACK PEPPER

6 FLOUR TORTILLAS
WARMED

PICANTE SAUCE
(PAGE 29)

MAKES 6 FAJITA TACOS

HEAT THE GRILL. Using a sharp knife, butterfly each flap by slicing in half lengthwise so that the two halves are barely joined. Grill over a hot fire for 12 to 15 minutes, or until well done. Season to taste with salt and pepper.

Transfer to a cutting board and chop against the grain into small pieces. Divide the meat evenly among the tortillas and top with the Picante Sauce.

Nuevo Tex-Mex Fajitas

THE PAPAYA-HABANERO SALSA NOT ONLY TASTES GOOD, BUT THE PAPAIN ENZYME PRESENT IN PAPAYA ACTS AS A NATURAL MEAT TENDERIZER. BECAUSE THE PAPAYA SEEDS ALSO CONTAIN PAPAIN, MANY FAMILIES IN MEXICO SAVE THE PAPAYA SEEDS WHEN THEY CLEAN THE FRUIT AND ADD THEM TO OTHER MARINADES. TRY THESE FAJITAS WITH REFRIED BEANS (PAGE 119) AND GRATED CHEESE OR WITH NUEVO GUACAMOLE (PAGE 78), SOUR CREAM, AND DICED TOMATOES.

USING A SHARP KNIFE, butterfly each flap by slicing in half lengthwise so that the two halves are barely joined. Place the meat in a nonreactive bowl with the salsa and turn to coat well. Cover and marinate for 4 hours in the refrigerator.

Heat the grill. Remove the meat from the salsa and season inside and out with salt to taste. Grill over a hot fire for 12 to 15 minutes, or until well done.

Transfer the meat to a cutting board and chop against the grain into small pieces. Place on a platter and serve with the tortillas and condiments of choice.

1 POUND FAJITA FLAP MEAT

PAPAYA-HABANERO SALSA
(PAGE 30)

SALT

8 FLOUR TORTILLAS
WARMED

MAKES 8 FAJITA TACOS

Rib-Eye Fajitas

THANKS TO A NATIONAL FAJITA CRAZE, THE PRICE OF FAJITA MEAT HAS TRIPLED IN THE LAST TEN YEARS. NOWADAYS, IT'S NOT MUCH MORE EXPENSIVE TO JUST GRILL A GOOD STEAK FOR YOUR TACOS. CHARCOAL-GRILLED STEAK TACOS ARE ACTUALLY KNOWN AS *TACOS AL CARBON*. NUEVO GUACAMOLE (PAGE 78), AND PICANTE SAUCE (PAGE 29) ARE THE FAVORITE CONDIMENTS.

4 RIB-EYE STEAKS
ABOUT 8 OUNCES EACH

2 CLOVES GARLIC
SLIVERED

1/4 CUP OLIVE OIL

2 TABLESPOONS GUAJILLO CHILE POWDER
(SEE PAGE 143)

SALT

LEMON WEDGES

12 FLOUR TORTILLAS
WARMED

MAKES **12** FAJITA TACOS

HEAT THE GRILL. Pierce the steaks with a knife in several places and insert the garlic slivers. In a bowl, combine the olive oil and guajillo chile powder and turn the steaks in the mixture until well coated. Season the steaks with salt and put them in a shallow dish while the coals are heating.

Grill the steaks over a fairly hot fire, turning once, for 4 to 6 minutes on each side, or to desired doneness.

Transfer the steaks to a cutting board and slice them against the grain into strips. Place on a platter and squeeze the lemon wedges over the top. Serve with the tortillas and condiments of choice.

Chipotle Swordfish Fajitas

THESE SPICY GRILLED FISH STRIPS TASTE GREAT WITH NUEVO GUACAMOLE (PAGE 78), BLACK BEAN RELISH (PAGE 121), AND SOUR CREAM.

HEAT THE GRILL. Combine the olive oil, chipotle puree, garlic, and lemon zest in a bowl. Season the swordfish steaks with salt and put them in a shallow dish. Spoon some of the marinade over them and let marinate for 10 minutes.

Remove the swordfish steaks from the marinade, reserving the marinade. Quickly grill the swordfish steaks over a fairly hot fire, turning once, for 2 to 4 minutes on each side, or to desired doneness. Drizzle the reserved marinade over the fish steaks as they cook.

Transfer the fish steaks to a cutting board and trim away the flesh from the bone. Slice into strips, being careful to remove any errant bones. Place the fish on a platter and squeeze the lemon wedges over the top. Serve with the tortillas and condiments of choice.

$1/2$ CUP EXTRA-VIRGIN OLIVE OIL

1 TABLESPOON CHIPOTLE PUREE
(SEE PAGE 144)

1 CLOVE GARLIC
MINCED

GRATED ZEST OF 1 LEMON

2 POUNDS SWORDFISH STEAKS
ABOUT $1/2$ INCH THICK

SALT

LEMON WEDGES

12 FLOUR TORTILLAS
WARMED

MAKES **12** FAJITA TACOS

Garlic Shrimp Fajitas

THE ONLY PROBLEM WITH GRILLED SHRIMP IS THAT YOU WAIT FOR TWENTY MINUTES TO HEAT THE GRILL AND THEN THE SHRIMP ARE DONE IN THE BLINK OF AN EYE. THAT'S WHY WE LIKE TO GRILL ANOTHER KIND OF MEAT AFTER THE SHRIMP ARE DONE, AND THE RIB-EYE FAJITAS (PAGE 110) ARE A GOOD PARTNER. THEN YOU CAN SERVE A TEX-MEX SURF-AND-TURF FAJITA DINNER. OR PAIR GARLIC SHRIMP FAJITAS WITH CHIPOTLE SWORDFISH FAJITAS (PAGE 111) FOR A SEAFOOD FAJITA FEAST. FRUITY SALSAS LIKE PINEAPPLE PICO (PAGE 35) ARE SENSATIONAL WITH THESE SHRIMP.

---

1 CUP (8 OUNCES) UNSALTED BUTTER
MELTED

2 SERRANO CHILES
STEMMED AND SEEDED, IF DESIRED

6 CLOVES GARLIC
MINCED

GRATED ZEST OF 1 LEMON

1 CUP FRESH PARSLEY LEAVES

2 POUNDS LARGE SHRIMP
PEELED AND DEVEINED

SALT

LEMON WEDGES

12 FLOUR TORTILLAS
WARMED

MAKES **12** FAJITA TACOS

HEAT THE GRILL. In a blender, combine the butter, serrano chiles, garlic, lemon zest, and parsley. Grind for about 10 seconds into a chunky paste. Transfer the paste to a bowl. Season the shrimp with salt and toss in the bowl with the paste until shrimp is well coated. Let marinate for 10 minutes.

Quickly grill the shrimp over a fairly hot fire, turning once, for about 2 minutes each side, or until just done.

Transfer the shrimp to a platter and garnish with lemon wedges. Serve with the tortillas and condiments of choice.

Note: If you are using smaller shrimp, thread them on wooden skewers to keep them from slipping through the grill. Plan on 4 to 5 shrimp for each skewer and soak the skewers in water first, so they don't burn on the grill.

Chicken Fajitas

GRILLING CHICKEN IS TRICKY, BUT GRILLING THESE BONELESS, SKINLESS CHICKEN BREASTS IS A PIECE OF CAKE. NUEVO GUACAMOLE (PAGE 78), RAJAS (SEE PAGE 143), AND CHIPOTLE SOUR CREAM (SEE CHICKEN-FRIED TUNA TACOS, PAGE 57) ARE OUR FAVORITE CONDIMENTS WITH THESE FAJITAS.

IN A BLENDER, combine the onion, Mexican oregano, lemon juice, and olive oil. Puree until smooth. Transfer the puree to a bowl and turn the chicken breasts in the mixture until well coated. Cover and marinate for about 4 hours in the refrigerator.

Heat the grill. Remove the chicken from the marinade and grill over a hot fire, turning once, for 2 minutes on each side. Then move the chicken to a cooler part of the grill, and cook, turning as needed, for 6 to 8 minutes, or until cooked through.

Transfer the chicken breasts to a cutting board and slice them against the grain into long strips. Place on a platter and bring to the table with the tortillas and condiments of choice.

1 WHITE ONION
QUARTERED

2 TABLESPOONS DRIED MEXICAN OREGANO

2 TABLESPOONS FRESH LEMON JUICE

4 BONELESS, SKINLESS
WHOLE CHICKEN BREASTS
ABOUT 7 OUNCES EACH

SALT

8 FLOUR TORTILLAS
WARMED

MAKES 8 FAJITA TACOS

CHAPTER 9

Sides of the Border

BeANS, RiCE, AND SiDE DiSHES

"ON THE OLDTIME RANCHES OF THE BORDER COUNTRY, WHERE I GREW UP, FRIJOLES WERE ABOUT AS REGULAR AS BREAD, AND IN SOME HOUSEHOLDS THEY STILL ARE."

— J. Frank Dobie, *A Taste of Texas* (1949)

J. Frank Dobie would be happy to know that beans are still as regular as bread along the border. Of course, they aren't the main course as often as they were in Dobie's time. But they're still there. No matter whether it's Tex-Mex, barbecue, or Southwestern cuisine, there are always beans on the table.

We've learned a lot about beans lately. We've learned to refry them with prosciutto and other exotic ingredients, to use black bean salads as a garnish, and to put them in salsas. But before we do any of those things to the beans, we enjoy a bowl all by themselves. J. Frank Dobie always insisted beans should be cooked plain and appreciated without a lot of extras. At his most extravagant, he would mash a couple of wild pequin chiles into his beans and top them with a little chopped onion.

When a fresh pot of beans is ready, it is the cook's privilege to eat the first bowl with nothing but a little salt and lot of cooking broth. In Mexico, a simple bowl of beans is sometimes served all by itself after the rest of the dinner. In Mexican and border cultures, such a bowl of beans is savored as a comfort food and treated with respect.

Texans inherited their reverence for *frijoles* from the Mexicans who taught the early cowboys how to cook. The Mexicans inherited their bean traditions from the Mesoamerican cultures of central Mexico. We often think of maize or corn as an early food of the native Americans, but the fact is that beans are much older. Beans were domesticated some ten thousand years ago. Corn came along five thousand years later.

The nearly religious regard for beans among Latin Americans has also resulted in some curious attitudes about which kind of beans you eat. Each Latin American microculture has its own bean and each regards others with disdain. The black turtle bean, which has become enormously popular in classy restaurants in the United States, is associated with poverty in parts of South America. Some Central Americans will eat no bean but the tiny red *coloradito*. In northern Mexico, pinto beans reign supreme.

Of course, Latinos are no more parochial about the color of their beans than Texans and Carolinians are about the color of their barbecue sauces. But luckily, while we've inherited a reverence for beans from Latin America, we haven't picked up their bean prejudices. The pinto bean is the dominant strain in the Southwest, but most of us will eat any beans we can find.

And we're finding more and more. Along with the black, white, red, and pinto beans found in most grocery stores, we have begun to see a new interest in heirloom beans in a rainbow of colors — beans that haven't been grown commercially in the United States for decades. These days, in specialty food stores, you can choose from twenty or more different kinds of beans in all shapes, sizes, and colors.

Try a few of these Nuevo Tex-Mex recipes on those designer beans or on some of your old favorites. But first, try them the old-fashioned way — without any frills.

Beans in Broth

SERVE FRESHLY MADE BEANS IN A BOWL LIKE A SOUP WITH PLENTY OF THE COOKING BROTH. YOU COULD GARNISH THEM WITH CHOPPED ONION, CHOPPED CHILES, SALSA, SOUR CREAM, OR TORTILLA WISPS (SEE PG 148) IF YOU WANTED TO SERVE THEM TO COMPANY. BUT IF YOU'RE ALL ALONE IN THE KITCHEN WITH A FRESH POT OF BEANS, YOU'LL PROBABLY JUST WANT TO EAT THEM PLAIN.

2 CUPS DRIED BEANS

6 CUPS WATER

1 GARLIC CLOVE
MINCED

1 OUNCE SALT PORK
(OPTIONAL)

SALT

MAKES $3\frac{1}{2}$ CUPS

PICK OVER THE BEANS, removing any stones or grit. Rinse the beans in a colander, drain well, and place in a large pan. Add the water and discard any beans that float to the surface. Bring to a boil over medium-high heat, reduce the heat to very low, and add the garlic and the salt pork, if using. Simmer gently, uncovered, for $1\frac{1}{2}$ to $2\frac{1}{2}$ hours, or until tender. (Some beans, such as black beans, may take longer.) Keep the level of the broth a good inch or so above the beans, adding more water as needed. Season the beans to taste with salt when they are done.

Epazote Beans: Add 2 fresh epazote sprigs to the beans. This Mexican herb is a favorite flavoring for beans, especially black beans, throughout Mexico. The strong herbal flavor is a nice accent, and epazote is also said to aid in the digestion of beans.

Black Beans with Plantains: Add 1 plantain, peeled and chopped, to the beans after they begin to boil. This will thicken the beans and add a tropical flavor.

Charro Beans: To a pot of cooked pinto beans, add 1 tablespoon guajillo chile powder (see page 144), $\frac{1}{2}$ teaspoon ground cumin, 4 slices bacon, fried crisp and crumbled and the bacon fat from the skillet, and $\frac{1}{2}$ cup Pico de Gallo (page 34).

Ranch Bean Soup: Remove half of the beans and puree them in a blender. (This will need to be done in several batches.) Return the pureed beans to the pot and add the same ingredients as for Charro Beans plus $1\frac{1}{2}$ cups chicken stock. Reheat and serve garnished with sour cream and tortilla wisps (see page 148).

THE
BEAN COOKING
DEBATE

Some people recommend that you soak beans overnight and change the water to aid digestibility. Most Mexican cooks insist that adding salt to the beans before they're done makes them tough. How much truth is there to any of this?

In an article in the Los Angeles Times, food editor Russ Parsons challenged these old nuggets of wisdom. According to Parsons, his own independent testing revealed that presoaking the beans didn't aid digestibility, but it did hurt the flavor and texture. He also said that salting the water while the beans were cooking had no effect on tenderness.

But according to the bean scientists at the California Dried Bean Advisory Board, if you presoak dried beans and then change the water, you make them more digestible by eliminating some of the oligiosaccharides that leach into the water during soaking. The Bean Board is curiously mum about the salt, but they claim that acids such as those present in tomatoes, chiles, and vinegar will slow the tenderizing process, so these ingredients should be added after the beans are cooked.

The debate between these two points of view reveals that cooking is still more of a subjective art than an exact science. Russ Parsons's article also points out that the more often you eat beans, the easier it is for your digestive system to adjust to them. Soaking may remove oligiosaccharides, but veteran bean eaters (like Russ Parsons) obviously don't have any problems with oligiosaccharides (whatever they are) anyway.

In our opinion, the first and most important thing to remember about the digestibility of beans is that you have to cook them until they're done. It's amazing how often people get impatient and eat the beans before they're ready. As for the salt, we thank Russ Parsons for finally proving what we have always suspected — that when you add the salt doesn't make any difference in the tenderness of the beans.

The biggest factor in the tenderness of beans isn't what you add to them, it's the age of the beans you're cooking. Old beans take longer to cook and the skin is always tougher. We still add the salt and spices after the beans are cooked anyway. Not because of the tenderness issue, but because it's easier to figure out how much to add after the beans are done and we can taste them.

Refried Beans

TRADITIONAL TEX-MEX *FRIJOLES REFRITOS* ARE FRIED IN LARD. WE DON'T REALLY HAVE ANYTHING AGAINST LARD. (CONTRARY TO POPULAR BELIEF, IT'S ACTUALLY LOWER IN CHOLESTEROL THAN MANY OTHER FATS, INCLUDING BUTTER.) BUT GOOD LARD IS HARD TO COME BY, SO WE USE VEGETABLE OIL. IF YOU HAVE SOME NICE FRESH LARD, FEEL FREE TO SUBSTITUTE IT. BACON DRIPPINGS ARE VERY TASTY, TOO (SEE VARIATIONS).

IN A MEDIUM-SIZED SKILLET, heat the oil over medium heat. Add the onion and sauté for 4 minutes, or until translucent. Add the garlic and sauté for 3 minutes longer. Add the beans and broth and mash with a potato masher. The beans should be partially crushed and thick. It isn't necessary to mash them completely smooth. If the beans are too pasty, add more broth. Season to taste with salt.

Serves 4 people.

Bacon Bean Refrito: Use any kind of cooked beans. Chop 4 slices of bacon and fry in the skillet until crispy. Remove the bacon with a slotted spoon to paper towels to drain. Proceed as directed, using the bacon fat in place of the oil. Add the crumbled bacon to the beans just before serving, or use it in another dish.

White Bean Refrito: Use cooked white navy beans. Add $1/2$ teaspoon ground cumin and $1/4$ teaspoon paprika to the sautéed onion and garlic and proceed as directed. Add $1/2$ cup chopped fresh cilantro after mashing the beans.

2 TABLESPOONS PEANUT OIL OR OTHER VEGETABLE OIL

$1/2$ ONION
FINELY CHOPPED

1 CLOVE GARLIC
MINCED

3 CUPS COOKED BEANS AND BROTH
(SEE PAGE 116)

SALT

MAKES ABOUT **3** CUPS

Black Bean and Prosciutto Refrito

THIS IS ONE THE RICHEST REFRIED BEAN RECIPES WE'VE EVER TRIED. WE CALL FOR IT IN LOTS OF OTHER RECIPES. IF YOU CAN'T BEAR TO USE PROSCIUTTO (IT'S VERY EXPENSIVE), SUBSTITUTE THIN SLICES OF THE BEST SMOKED HAM YOU CAN AFFORD.

1½ TABLESPOONS PEANUT OIL

¼ CUP CHOPPED ONION

1 CLOVE GARLIC
MINCED

¼ CUP JULIENNED PROSCIUTTO

3 CUPS COOKED BLACK BEANS
AND BROTH
(SEE PAGE 116)

3 PICKLED JALAPEÑOS
STEMMED, SEEDED, AND DICED

SALT

MAKES 3½ CUPS

IN A SKILLET, heat the peanut oil over medium heat. Add the onion and sauté for 4 minutes, or until translucent. Add the garlic and prosciutto and sauté for 3 minutes longer. Add the beans and broth and the jalapeños and mash with a potato masher. The beans should be partially crushed and thick. It isn't necessary to mash them completely smooth. Cook the beans over low heat for 3 minutes longer, until well blended. If the beans are too pasty, add more broth. Season to taste with salt.

Serves 6-8 people.

Black Bean Relish

THE IDEA OF USING BLACK BEANS IN A RELISH IS COMPLETELY FOREIGN TO THE LATIN AMERICAN CULTURES WHERE BLACK BEANS ARE EATEN. BUT THERE'S NO DENYING THEY MAKE A DRAMATIC-LOOKING GARNISH OVER FISH OR POULTRY, OR IN COMBINATION WITH OTHER VEGETABLES. THE TRICK HERE IS TO KEEP THE BEANS WHOLE AND PERFECT LOOKING, WHILE AT THE SAME TIME BEING SURE THEY ARE THOROUGHLY COOKED.

IN A BOWL, COMBINE THE BEANS, olive oil, tomato, lemon juice, and cilantro. Toss well. Season to taste with salt. Refrigerate until ready to use.

1 CUP COOKED BLACK BEANS
DRAINED AND RINSED
(SEE PAGE 116)

2 TABLESPOONS OLIVE OIL

$1/2$ CUP DICED TOMATO

1 TABLESPOON FRESH LEMON JUICE

2 TABLESPOONS CHOPPED
FRESH CILANTRO

SALT

MAKES ABOUT $1\frac{1}{2}$ CUPS

Nuevo Tex-Mex Rice

IN MEXICAN COOKING, RICE IS ALWAYS SAUTÉED IN OIL WITH SOME FLAVORINGS BEFORE THE LIQUID IS ADDED. THIS NOT ONLY BOOSTS THE FLAVOR, BUT IT ALSO KEEPS THE KERNELS FROM STICKING TOGETHER. FOR OUR RECIPES, WE ALWAYS USE TEXMATI RICE, A HYBRID OF LONG-GRAIN RICE AND ONE OF THE WORLD'S BEST RICES, INDIAN BASMATI. IT IS EXCEPTIONALLY NUTTY TASTING AND FIRM AND HOLDS UP WELL TO SAUTÉING, BUT IT DOESN'T COST AS MUCH AS BASMATI. YOU CAN SUBSTITUTE BASMATI OR LONG-GRAIN WHITE RICE IF YOU WANT.

1¼ CUPS TEXMATI RICE

3 TABLESPOONS OLIVE OIL

3 CLOVES GARLIC
CHOPPED

¼ ONION
FINELY DICED

2 SERRANO CHILES
STEMMED AND MINCED

2½ CUPS WATER

2 BAY LEAVES

1 TABLESPOON UNSALTED BUTTER

SALT

MAKES ABOUT 3 CUPS

RINSE THE RICE BRIEFLY in cold water and drain. In a saucepan, heat the olive oil over medium heat. Add the garlic, onion, serrano chiles, and rice and sauté for 7 to 10 minutes, or until the rice turns opaque.

Add the water, bay leaves, butter, and salt to taste. Bring to a boil, cover, reduce the heat to low, and cook for about 20 minutes, or until the liquid is absorbed and the rice is tender.

Serves 4–6 people.

Oven Method: Preheat an oven to 350 degrees F. Start the rice in an ovenproof saucepan on the stove top. When the water comes to a boil, cover the pan and place it in the oven for 20 minutes, or until the rice is tender. Cooking the rice in the oven reduces the risk of burning it. Let the rice sit, covered, for 5 minutes before serving. Season to taste with salt.

Bock Rice: Substitute 1 bottle (12 ounces) dark beer for 1½ cups of the water.

Mexican Marigold Mint Rice: Add 2 tablespoons chopped fresh Mexican marigold mint to the rice after it is cooked, mixing carefully so as not to crush the kernels.

Spicy Rice: Substitute 1 cup Picante Sauce (page 29) for 1 cup of the water.

Vanilla Rice

THE AROMA OF THIS RICE IS INTOXICATING. IT IS A WONDERFUL SIDE DISH WITH SWEET SAUCES OR DELICATE FISH DISHES.

RINSE THE RICE IN COLD WATER and drain. In a saucepan, heat the oil over medium heat. Add serrano chiles, onion, celery, and carrots and sauté for 3 to 5 minutes, or until the onion is translucent.

Using the tip of a knife, scrape the seeds from the vanilla bean halves into the pan. (If using vanilla extract, add with the stock.) Then add the rice and stir for 3 to 5 minutes, or until the rice grains are coated with the oil. Add the chicken stock and bring to a boil. Cover, reduce the heat to low, and cook for 20 minutes, or until the liquid is absorbed and the rice is tender. Season to taste with salt.

Serves 4–6 people.

Note: The oven method described on page 122 can be used for this recipe as well.

1$\frac{1}{2}$ CUPS TEXMATI RICE, BASMATI RICE, OR OTHER LONG-GRAIN WHITE RICE

3 TABLESPOONS VEGETABLE OIL

2 SERRANO CHILES
STEMMED AND FINELY CHOPPED

$\frac{1}{2}$ ONION
FINELY CHOPPED

1 CELERY STALK
FINELY CHOPPED

1 CARROT
PEELED AND FINELY CHOPPED

1 VANILLA BEAN, SPLIT LENGTHWISE, OR
$\frac{1}{2}$ TEASPOON PURE VANILLA EXTRACT

3 CUPS CHICKEN STOCK

SALT

MAKES ABOUT 3$\frac{1}{2}$ CUPS

Annatto Rice with Wild Mushrooms

BRIGHT ORANGE RICE AND SILKY WILD MUSHROOMS ARE AN EXCEPTIONAL COMBINATION THAT WILL LIGHT UP ANY PLATE. TRY IT WITH A MOLE DISH LIKE CHICKEN MOLE TEJANO (PAGE 95).

1 CUP TEXMATI RICE, BASMATI RICE, OR OTHER LONG-GRAIN WHITE RICE

½ CUP ANNATTO OIL
(SEE ANCHIOTE PASTE PAGE 142)

2 CLOVES GARLIC
MINCED

½ ONION
FINELY DICED

1 SMALL CARROT
PEELED AND FINELY DICED

1 CELERY STALK
FINELY DICED

1½ CUPS WILD MUSHROOMS
SUCH AS MORELS OR CHANTERELLES
THINLY SLICED

FRESH CORN KERNELS
FROM 1 EAR OF CORN

1 TEASPOON GROUND CINNAMON

2½ CUPS CHICKEN STOCK

SALT

MAKES ABOUT 2½ CUPS

RINSE THE RICE BRIEFLY in cold water and drain. In a large saucepan, heat the annatto oil over medium heat. Add the garlic, onion, carrot, and celery and sauté for 2 minutes. Add the mushrooms and corn and sauté for 4 to 6 minutes, or until the onion is translucent and the mushrooms are tender. Add the rice and cinnamon and stir for 1 to 2 minutes, or until the rice is well coated with the oil.

Heat the chicken stock to a boil, add it to the rice mixture, and reduce the heat to low. Cook, uncovered, for 20 minutes, or until the liquid is absorbed and the rice is tender. Season to taste with salt.

Serves 4-6 people.

Note: The oven method described on page 122 can be used for this recipe as well.

Ancho chiles Stuffed with Sweet Potato

THE COMBINATION OF SWEET AND HOT FLAVORS MAKES THIS A SPECTACULAR SIDE DISH WITH ROASTED PORK OR TURKEY. THE SWEET POTATOES BRING OUT THE DRIED-FRUIT FLAVORS IN THE ANCHOS, BUT THE HEAT OF THE CHILES WILL SURPRISE YOU.

PLACE THE ANCHO CHILES in a bowl and add hot water to cover. Let stand for 20 minutes, or until softened but not falling apart. Preheat an oven to 350 degrees F.

In a small skillet, melt the butter over medium heat. Add the onion and sauté for 2 to 3 minutes, or until wilted. Add the raisins and brown sugar and stir to dissolve the sugar. Transfer to a bowl. Add the sweet potatoes and mash well. You should have almost 3 cups. Add the garlic puree, cinnamon, thyme, pecans, and salt to taste.

Drain the chiles and slit each one along one side. Carefully remove the seeds, leaving the stem intact. (If you want to cut down on the heat level, also try and scrape out as much of the pale-colored membrane surrounding the seeds and stem as possible.) Spoon an equal amount of the sweet potato mixture into each pepper. (A normal-sized ancho will hold about $1/2$ cup.) Place slit-side up on a greased baking sheet. Place the stuffed peppers in the oven for 6 to 8 minutes, or until piping hot.

Garnish with sour cream before serving.

4 ANCHO CHILES

4 TABLESPOONS BUTTER

$1/2$ CUP CHOPPED ONION

$3/4$ CUP RAISINS

2 TABLESPOONS BROWN SUGAR

1 LARGE SWEET POTATO
PEELED, BOILED UNTIL
TENDER, AND DRAINED

2 TABLESPOONS ROASTED GARLIC PUREE
(SEE PAGE 145)

$1/2$ TEASPOON GROUND CINNAMON

1 TEASPOON DRIED THYME

$1/2$ CUP PECANS
TOASTED AND CHOPPED

SALT

SOUR CREAM

MAKES 4 STUFFED PEPPERS

Roasted Potatoes with Garlic and Mexican Oregano

RED POTATOES ARE THE MOST COMMON POTATOES IN MEXICAN COOKING. THEY DON'T MASH VERY WELL, BUT THEY ARE EXCELLENT ROASTED.

1/2 CUP OLIVE OIL

3 POUNDS RED POTATOES
QUARTERED

3 CLOVES GARLIC
MINCED

1/2 ONION
CHOPPED

1 TABLESPOON GROUND
DRIED MEXICAN OREGANO

1/4 CUP SHERRY VINEGAR

SALT

SERVES 6 PEOPLE

PREHEAT AN OVEN TO 375 DEGREES F. In a bowl, toss together the olive oil, potatoes, garlic, onion, oregano, and vinegar. Transfer to a baking pan in which the potatoes fit in a single layer.

Place in the oven for 35 to 45 minutes, or until the potatoes are crisp and brown. Add salt to taste just before serving.

Coca-Cola Habanero Potatoes

KEEP AN EYE ON THE SAUCE AND KEEP THE HEAT LOW, AS THE SUGAR BURNS EASILY. THESE SWEET-HOT POTATOES ARE DELIGHTFUL WITH DISHES THAT FEATURE A TART TOMATILLO SAUCE SUCH AS DUCK BREAST IN GREEN MOLE (PAGE 98).

IN A SKILLET, combine the butter, potatoes, onion, and garlic over low heat. Cook, stirring often, for 15 minutes, or until the onions begin to caramelize. Add the habanero chile and the Coca-Cola and cook slowly for 15 to 20 minutes, or until the potatoes are tender. If the liquid starts to cook away before the potatoes are done, add a little water. The liquid should be reduced to a light syrup. Season to taste with salt.

Transfer the potatoes to a serving bowl and spoon the liquid over the top.

1 TABLESPOON UNSALTED BUTTER

4 YUKON GOLD POTATOES OR SIMILAR YELLOW-FLESHED POTATOES, ABOUT 3 POUNDS TOTAL
CUT INTO 1/2-INCH PIECES

1/2 ONION
CHOPPED

2 CLOVES GARLIC
CHOPPED

1/2 HABANERO CHILE
SEEDED AND MINCED

2 CUPS COCA-COLA

SALT

SERVES 4~6 PEOPLE

Ice Cream or Flan?

NUeVO TEX~mEX DEsSeRTs

CHAPTER 10

WHEN WE THINK OF TEX-MEX DESSERTS, WE ALWAYS THINK OF AUSTIN'S EL PATIO RESTAURANT. THAT'S PROBABLY BECAUSE it's the only Tex-Mex joint where we ever eat dessert. And we only eat dessert at El Patio because they still carry on that quaint custom of including dessert with your dinner. ❧ As one of the old school Tex-Mex joints, El Patio has become a sort of Tex-Mex museum. It hasn't changed much since it opened in 1954, and neither have the desserts. With your combination platter, you get your choice of a tiny scoop of sherbet or a praline. With this sort of selection, it's no wonder that people seldom bother with dessert at a Tex-Mex restaurant.

The biggest innovation to hit the dessert list in Tex-Mex restaurants in the last twenty years has been the Mexican caramel custard called flan. (The pralines are still sold at the cash register, but they don't make the dessert list much anymore.) Should you ask about dessert, your waiter or waitress will recite your options in the form of a question: "Ice cream or flan?"

Staying true to the tradition, we've come up with some Nuevo Tex-Mex ice creams and flans. Well, okay, we cheated a little. We whipped up some ancho chile brownies because they go so well with the ice cream. We also put some of the ice creams into big, beautiful sundaes like the Nuevo Tex-Mex Banana Split. Oh, and we've added a couple of dessert sauces like Strawberry-Raspberry Mint Salsa, so you have something to put on your sundaes.

Actually you can use the dessert sauces on your flan, too. In fact, wait until you try the Chocolate Almond Sauce on your flan.

So what'll it be? Ice cream or flan?

Vanilla Bean Ice Cream

HERE'S OUR BASIC ICE CREAM RECIPE. THE WHOLE VANILLA BEAN MAKES A HUGE DIFFERENCE, SO TRY HARD TO FIND ONE! THE VARIATION WITH CORN MAY SOUND STRANGE, BUT IT'S ONE OF THE RICHEST ICE CREAMS WE'VE EVER HAD — AND THE NUEVO TEX-MEX BANANA SPLIT (PAGE 139) JUST AIN'T THE SAME WITHOUT IT.

1³/₄ CUPS WHOLE MILK

1¹/₃ CUPS WHIPPING CREAM

¹/₂ VANILLA BEAN, SPLIT LENGTHWISE, OR
1 TEASPOON PURE VANILLA EXTRACT

¹/₂ CUP SUGAR

3 TABLESPOONS MAPLE SYRUP

9 EGG YOLKS

MAKES 1 QUART

IN A MEDIUM-SIZED SAUCEPAN, combine the milk, cream, vanilla bean, sugar, and maple syrup. Place over low heat, bring to a simmer, and simmer gently for 3 minutes, or until the sugar is dissolved. Remove from the heat and discard the vanilla bean.

Place the egg yolks in a bowl and whisk until well blended. Slowly stir the hot cream mixture into the egg yolks, and then return to the saucepan. Simmer over very low heat, stirring constantly, for 5 minutes, or until the mixture thickens slightly. Remove from heat, let cool, and chill before freezing. Freeze in an ice cream maker according to the manufacturer's instructions.

Corn Ice Cream: Add 2 cups fresh corn kernels to the milk mixture and heat as directed. After removing the vanilla bean, transfer the mixture to a blender and puree until smooth. Strain the mixture into the eggs to remove any remaining kernel hulls. Proceed as directed.

Pumpkin Flan

THIS IS OUR FAVORITE AUTUMN DESSERT. IF YOU LIKE PUMPKIN PIE, YOU'LL LOVE THIS LIGHTER ALTERNATIVE.

PREHEAT AN OVEN TO 350 DEGREES F. Butter six ³/₄ cup ramekins and coat with sugar. In a medium-sized saucepan combine the condensed milk and regular milk and cook over medium heat for 5 minutes or until scalded.

In a nonreactive bowl, beat the eggs and yolk lightly. Add the vanilla, sugar and spices and whisk until well mixed. While continuing to whisk, add the milk gradually and then the pumpkin. Fill the buttered and sugared ramekins with the mixture.

Place the ramekins in a baking pan and add hot water to the pan to reach halfway up the sides of the molds. Cover the pan with aluminum foil and bake for 1 hour and 15 minutes or until the custards are set. Remove from the oven and let cool. Run a paring knife around the inside edge of each mold to loosen the custards. Then unmold onto 6 small plates.

1 CUP CONDENSED MILK

1 CUP MILK

4 EGGS, PLUS 1 EGG YOLK

1 TEASPOON PURE VANILLA EXTRACT

1 TABLESPOON SUGAR

¹/₈ TEASPOON GROUND NUTMEG

PINCH OF CINNAMON ALLSPICE

PINCH OF GROUND CLOVES

1 CUP CANNED UNSWEETENED PUMPKIN

6 BUTTERED AND SUGARED RAMEKINS

SERVES 6 PEOPLE

Shown with Mango Habanero Whipped Cream (page 141).

Flan

SINCE WE LIKE TO TOP OUR FLAN WITH DESSERT SAUCES, THIS ONE IS MADE WITHOUT THE CUSTOMARY CARAMEL TOPPING. ALL BY ITSELF, IT IS ONE OF THE LIGHTEST AND MOST DELICATE DESSERTS IMAGINABLE.

4 CUPS (1 QUART) WHOLE MILK

1¼ CUPS SUGAR

1 VANILLA BEAN, SPLIT LENGTHWISE
(SEE PAGE 148)

4 EGGS

6 EGG YOLKS

SERVES **12** PEOPLE

PREHEAT AN OVEN TO 350 DEGREES F. Butter twelve ³/₄-cup ramekins. In a medium-sized saucepan, combine the milk and sugar. Using the tip of a knife, scrape the seeds from the vanilla bean into the pan. Place over low heat and heat, stirring, for about 10 minutes, or until small bubbles break along the edges of the pan and the sugar is dissolved. Remove from the heat and let cool.

In a nonreactive bowl, beat the eggs lightly. Stir the milk mixture into the eggs. Strain through a fine-mesh sieve into a pitcher, then pour into the prepared ramekins.

Place the ramekins in a baking pan and add hot water to the pan to reach halfway up the sides of the molds. Cover the pan with aluminum foil and bake for 35 to 45 minutes, or until the custards are set. Remove from the oven and let cool. Run a paring knife around the inside edge of each mold to loosen the custards. Then unmold onto 12 small plates.

Cranberry-Star Anise Flan: Add 2 whole star anise to the milk with the vanilla. Discard them when the mixture is cool. Place 8 fresh cranberries into each ramekin before adding the custard mixture. Proceed as directed.

Strawberry-Raspberry Mint Salsa

RASPBERRY PUREE, SLICED STRAWBERRIES, AND A LITTLE MINT MAKE A REFRESHINGLY TART SALSA THAT GOES GREAT WITH ICE CREAM, FLAN, OR CHEESECAKE.

IN A BLENDER, combine the raspberries, water, lemon juice, and sugar. Puree until smooth. Strain through a fine-mesh sieve into a bowl. Add the strawberries and mint and toss to combine. Cover and chill before serving.

1 CUP RASPBERRIES

1/2 CUP WATER

1 1/2 TEASPOONS FRESH LEMON JUICE

1 1/2 TABLESPOONS SUGAR

1 CUP SLICED STRAWBERRIES

1 TEASPOON CHOPPED FRESH MINT

MAKES 1 1/2 CUPS

Pecan Cookies

TO GIVE YOUR DESSERTS A SOUTHWESTERN LOOK, CUT THESE COOKIES INTO BIG CACTUS SHAPES AND STICK THEM IN YOUR ICE CREAM. WE ALSO LIKE TO USE OUR TEXAS-SHAPED COOKIE CUTTERS ON THESE.

³/₄ CUP ALL-PURPOSE FLOUR

³/₄ CUP CAKE FLOUR

1 CUP CONFECTIONERS' SUGAR

1 CUP PECANS
TOASTED AND FINELY CHOPPED

¹/₂ CUP FIRMLY PACKED BROWN SUGAR

³/₄ CUP UNSALTED BUTTER
SOFTENED

1 EGG YOLK

1 TEASPOON PURE VANILLA EXTRACT

MAKES ABOUT **12** LARGE COOKIES

PREHEAT AN OVEN TO 325 DEGREES F. Butter a baking sheet.

In a bowl, stir together the flours, confectioners' sugar, and pecans. In another bowl, combine the brown sugar and butter and beat with an electric mixer on high speed until creamy. Beat in the egg yolk and vanilla. Reduce the speed to medium and slowly add the flour mixture, beating until fully incorporated and a dough forms. Gather into a ball, wrap in plastic wrap, and chill for 10 to 15 minutes.

On a floured work surface, roll out the dough ¹/₂ inch thick. Cut into desired shapes with a cookie cutter or a knife. Gather up the scraps, reroll, and cut out additional cookies. Arrange the cookies on the prepared pan.

Place in the oven and bake for 10 to 12 minutes, or until light brown. Remove from the oven and let cool for 1 minute before removing from the baking sheet with a spatula. Serve warm. The cookies will keep in a tightly covered container for up to 3 days.

Rebecca's Ancho-Pine Nut Brownies

REBECCA RATHER IS ONE OF AUSTIN'S BEST BAKERS, AND THIS IS ONE OF HER FAVORITE BROWNIE RECIPES. TRY THESE WHILE THEY'RE STILL WARM WITH A SCOOP OF VANILLA BEAN ICE CREAM (PAGE 130).

PREHEAT AN OVEN TO 325 DEGREES F. Butter a 9- by 13-inch baking pan. In the top pan of a double boiler, combine the chocolate and butter. Place over barely simmering water in the bottom pan and heat, stirring occasionally, until the chocolate and butter have melted and are combined. Remove from the heat.

In a bowl, whisk together the eggs and sugar until thick and smooth. Slowly pour into the chocolate mixture, stirring constantly. Stir in the flour, ancho chile powder, chocolate morsels, and pine nuts. Pour evenly into the prepared baking pan.

Place in the oven and bake for 20 to 25 minutes, or until a knife inserted in the center comes out clean. Remove from the oven and let cool completely. Cut into squares to serve.

1 POUND SEMISWEET CHOCOLATE
COARSELY CHOPPED

1 POUND UNSALTED BUTTER
CUT INTO SMALL PIECES

8 EGGS

3 CUPS SUGAR

2 CUPS ALL-PURPOSE FLOUR

1 1/2 TABLESPOONS
ANCHO CHILE POWDER
(SEE PAGE 143)

1 CUP SEMISWEET CHOCOLATE MORSELS

1 CUP PINE NUTS
TOASTED

MAKES 12 LARGE BROWNIES

Chocolate Corn Sticks

THERE ISN'T ANY CORN IN THESE CORN STICKS. WE JUST CALL THEM THAT BECAUSE WE BAKE THEM IN AN OLD-FASHIONED CORN-STICK MOLD. TRY SOME WARM WITH MANGO-HABANERO WHIPPED CREAM (PAGE 141).

1 1/2 CUPS (12 OUNCES)
UNSALTED BUTTER

1 1/2 POUNDS BITTERSWEET CHOCOLATE
COARSELY CHOPPED

9 EGGS
SEPARATED

1/2 CUP FIRMLY PACKED BROWN SUGAR

1/4 VANILLA BEAN
SPLIT LENGTHWISE (SEE PAGE 148)

1 TEASPOON PURE VANILLA EXTRACT

1 TABLESPOON COFFEE
EXTRACT OR ESPRESSO

PINCH OF SEA SALT

1 CUP ALMONDS
TOASTED AND GROUND

MAKES 8 CORN STICKS

PREHEAT AN OVEN TO 425 DEGREES F. In the top pan of a double boiler, combine the butter and chocolate. Place over barely simmering water in the bottom pan and heat, stirring constantly, until the chocolate and butter have melted and are combined. Remove from the heat and set aside in a warm spot.

In a nonreactive bowl, whisk together the egg yolks and brown sugar until thick and smooth. Pour into the chocolate mixture and mix well. Using the tip of a knife, scrape the vanilla seeds into the bowl. Add the vanilla extract, coffee extract, and salt, mixing well. Fold in half of the almonds and set aside.

Place the egg whites in another bowl and place over the lower pan of the double boiler to warm slightly. Using a mixer with a whip attachment, whip the egg whites until soft peaks form. Fold a small amount of the egg whites into the chocolate mixture to lighten it, then fold in the remaining just until no white streaks remain. Sprinkle the remaining almonds into an 8-mold cast-iron corn-stick pan. Pour the batter evenly over the almonds.

Place in the oven for 15 minutes, or until a toothpick inserted near the edge comes out clean. Remove from the oven and let cool completely. Using a knife, gently remove the corn sticks.

Nuevo Tex-Mex Banana Split

YOU MAY USE ANY KIND OF ICE CREAM YOU WANT FOR THIS RECIPE, BUT THE SWEET CORN ICE CREAM WORKS LIKE MAGIC WITH CHOCOLATE, ALMONDS, AND BANANAS. TOP IT ALL OFF WITH WHIPPED CREAM, IF YOU LIKE.

STIR TOGETHER the sugar and cinnamon on a plate. Roll the banana halves in the mixture, coating evenly. In a medium-sized skillet, melt the butter over medium heat. Add the banana halves and cook, turning as needed, until lightly browned on all sides.

Transfer 2 banana halves to each plate. Position 3 scoops of ice cream between each pair of banana halves. Spoon the Chocolate Almond sauce over the middle scoop and the Strawberry-Raspberry Salsa over the other 2 scoops.

2 TABLESPOONS CONFECTIONERS' SUGAR

1 TABLESPOON GROUND CINNAMON

4 RIPE BANANAS
PEELED AND CUT IN HALF LENGTHWISE

1 TABLESPOON UNSALTED BUTTER

1 QUART SWEET CORN ICE CREAM
(PAGE 130)

1 CUP CHOCOLATE ALMOND SAUCE
HEATED (PAGE 140)

2 CUPS STRAWBERRY-RASPBERRY MINT SALSA
(PAGE 135)

SERVES 4 PEOPLE

Chocolate Almond Sauce

AN OLD-FASHIONED CHOCOLATE FUDGE SUNDAE TASTES EVEN BETTER WITH THIS HOMEMADE CHOCOLATE SAUCE. USE THE BEST-QUALITY CHOCOLATE YOU CAN FIND!

12 OUNCES SEMISWEET CHOCOLATE
COARSELY CHOPPED

1/2 CUP ALMONDS
TOASTED AND CRUSHED

5 TABLESPOONS WHIPPING CREAM

1/2 CUP WATER

MAKES ABOUT **2** CUPS

IN THE TOP PAN OF A DOUBLE BOILER, combine the chocolate, almonds, cream, and water. Place over barely simmering water in the bottom pan and heat, stirring constantly, until the chocolate is melted. Use immediately, or set aside in a warm spot.

To reheat, place the chocolate in a saucepan over very low heat, stirring constantly until melted and warm.

Mango-Habanero Whipped Cream

SWEET AND HOT IS A COMBINATION THAT SOUNDS ODD, BUT QUICKLY BECOMES ADDICTIVE. THIS SWEET AND HOT WHIPPED CREAM GOES EXCEPTIONALLY WELL WITH CHOCOLATE.

IN A SMALL SAUCEPAN, combine the wine and sugar and bring to a boil, stirring to dissolve the sugar. Reduce the heat to low and simmer for 3 minutes to form a syrupy consistency. Remove from the heat and let cool.

In a blender, combine the mango pulp, habanero chile, and wine syrup and blend until smooth. Transfer to a bowl, cover, and refrigerate until well chilled.

In a chilled bowl, whip the cream until stiff peaks form. Fold the cream into the chilled mango mixture. Use immediately.

1/4 CUP DRY WHITE WINE

1/4 CUP SUGAR

1 RIPE MANGO
PEELED AND PITTED

1/4 HABANERO CHILE
SEEDED

1 1/2 CUPS WHIPPING CREAM

SERVES 8 PEOPLE

ACHIOTE PASTE ❧ ❧ ❧ Achiote paste is made from ground annatto seeds, which come from a tropical tree of the same name. Sometimes it is a combination of the ground seeds and other spices. It is a favorite seasoning throughout Mexico and especially in the Yucatán. Annatto seeds turn foods a bright orange. In fact, they are used to color Cheddar cheese.

According to many cookbooks, you can grind annatto seeds in a coffee grinder to make your own achiote paste. We haven't had any luck with this. Annatto seeds are so hard that after 10 minutes of grinding, we seldom get more than a little dust. We've also heard that soaking the seeds in water overnight helps. But we suggest that you forget about making achiote paste and buy yours already made at a Mexican market. If you can find annatto seeds, but can't find achiote paste, you can make annatto oil, which will give food the same color without the grinding problem: Combine $1/4$ cup annatto seeds and $1/2$ cup of vegetable oil in a small pan and place over very low heat. Cook for 15 minutes, or until the oil turns orange. Strain the oil and discard the seeds.

CHILE PEPPERS ❧ ❧ ❧ We often use the words *chiles* and *peppers* interchangeably in the Southwest, but we often use them together, too. One reason for the popularity of the redundant term *chile peppers* is that the words *chili* and *chile* refer to specific dishes in Texas and New Mexico. "Chili" means chili con carne, but it is actually an alternate spelling of "chile" and is pronounced the same in English. Texas writer and naturalist J. Frank Dobie used the "chili" spelling to refer to both the peppers and the dish. Pepper expert Dr. Jean Andrews, author of *Peppers: the Domesticated Capsicums*, advocates the English spelling, "chilli."

Dallas columnist Frank X. Tolbert, who started the Terlingua chili cook-off, fought a humorous war with New Mexico over the spelling of the word. Chile in New Mexico means a pepper, but it also means green chile stew. Chile peppers may be a redundant term, but the redundancy is often necessary to make it clear that you are talking about the pods and not a specific dish.

Fresh Chiles Fresh chile peppers are usually harvested in the green stage. Fully ripened, red chiles are most often used for drying, but they also sometimes turn up fresh in the supermarket. Green or red chiles can be used interchangeably unless the recipe specifies one or the other. The following fresh chile peppers, listed from mildest to hottest, appear in this book:

ANAHEIM Also known as the long green chile by New Mexicans (until it turns red and becomes the long red chile), the Anaheim has a pleasant vegetable flavor and ranges from slightly warm to medium-hot on the heat scale. Anaheims are generally roasted and peeled before they are used. The name comes from a chile cannery opened by a farmer named Emilio Ortega in Anaheim, California, in 1900. Since Ortega brought the pepper seeds to California from New Mexico, most New Mexicans feel the name is a misnomer. We call them Anaheims because, in the spirit of Frank X. Tolbert, we love to irritate New Mexicans, and because, outside of New Mexico, when you ask for a long green chile at the grocery store, there is no telling what you'll get.

POBLANO Fatter and wider than the Anaheim, the poblano is a darker green and has a richer flavor. It is one of the most commonly used chiles in Mexican cooking, both in its fresh and dried form (see ancho). Poblanos are named after the Mexican city of Puebla, where they probably originated. They are generally slightly hot and are usually roasted and peeled before use.

JALAPEÑO Hot, green, and bullet shaped, the jalapeño is the classic Tex-Mex hot pepper and one of the world's best-known chiles. Originally grown in Mexico, it is named for Jalapa, a town in the state of Veracruz. The fresh jalapeño has a strong, vegetal flavor to go with the heat. We prefer to cook with fresh jalapeños, but the jalapeño is most widely consumed in its pickled form. Besides hot sauce, a bowl of pickled jalapeños is the most popular condiment on the Tex-Mex table.

SERRANOS Similar to the jalapeño, the serrano is hotter and smaller. Most Mexicans claim that serranos have a fuller, more herbaceous flavor. Since the vast majority of jalapeños are pickled, the serrano is actually the most widely used fresh chile pepper in Mexico and Texas.

PEQUIN Also known as *piquin, chilipiquin,* or *chiltepin,* this tiny chile grows wild throughout southern Texas and northern Mexico. Although pequin seems to be a corruption of the Spanish *pequeño,* meaning "small," the Spanish name itself is probably a corruption of *chiltecpin,* a Nahuatl word meaning flea chile, a reference to both its size and its sting. Since they were spread by birds rather than cultivation, experts tell us that pequins are the oldest chiles in North America. In northern Mexico, they are collected in the wild and sold in markets, where they fetch more than almost any other chile. They are sometimes dried and preserved for year-round use. A pequin bush can be found in almost any backyard or vacant lot in south Texas, and pequins are therefore very common in Tex-Mex home cooking. Because they are not grown commercially, they are seldom found in restaurant cooking or in grocery stores. If you find some, you can substitute 3 or 4 fresh pequins for 1 serrano or $1/2$ a jalapeño.

HABANERO The world's hottest pepper, the habanero should be treated with respect. It has a wonderful apricotlike flavor and aroma, but must be used in small quantities and handled with care. The habanero came to Mexico from the Caribbean and is named after Havana, Cuba.

Roasting Fresh Peppers Place the whole fresh pepper directly over a high gas flame and turn the pepper as needed to blister the skin on all sides. Don't allow the flame to burn too long in one place or you'll burn through the pepper. After most of the skin has been well blistered, wrap the warm pepper in a wet paper towel and set it aside to steam gently. When you remove the towel, most of the skin should come off with it. Scrape off the rest of the skin with a butter knife.

If you don't have a gas range, put the pepper in a skillet with 2 tablespoons vegetable oil and blister it over high heat on an electric burner. Then wrap it in a wet paper towel and proceed as directed.

RAJAS Roasted peppers that have been seeded, peeled, and cut into strips are called rajas. You'll find them called for in some recipes and as a condiment for fajitas.

Dried Chiles The following dried chile peppers, listed from mildest to hottest, are used in this book:

ANCHO The dried form of the poblano chile, the ancho is dark brown and wide. (In fact, the word *ancho* means "wide" in Spanish.) Anchos are the fleshiest of the dried chiles, and their pulp combines a little bitter flavor with a sweetness reminiscent of raisins. They are usually mild, although occasionally one will surprise you with its heat.

GUAJILLO Tapered, with a smooth, shiny, reddish skin, the guajillo has a tart and medium-hot flavor. When soaked and pureed, it gives foods an orange color. Dried Anaheims are also sometimes called guajillos, but they are much milder.

PASILLA Long and skinny with a black, slightly wrinkled skin, the pasilla has a strong, satisfying flavor and can range from medium-hot to hot. The name comes from the Spanish *pasa,* meaning "raisin," a reference to the appearance of the skin.

CHIPOTLE This is the smoke-dried jalapeño. Small, wrinkled, and light brown, chipotles have an incredibly rich, smoky flavor and are usually very hot. Smoking is a method of preserving jalapeños that was already common in Mexico when the Spanish first arrived. The original Nahuatl spelling, *chilpotle,* is also sometimes seen.

We prefer to use dried chipotles, but you can also buy them canned. Canned chipotles are acceptable in most recipes. Obviously, you can't make chile powder from canned chipotles, but you can use them for purees. Canned chipotles are already soaked in some kind of sauce, usually the vinegary adobo sauce. Just stem and seed them and puree them with some of the sauce from the can.

Making Chile Powders Several of the recipes in this book call for various chile powders. The chile powders sold in most grocery stores contain other spices and are often so dried out that the powder yields little flavor. They also tend to give sauces and chili con carne a gritty texture. You are much better off making chile powders at home in an electric coffee grinder. This also allows you to use such flavorful peppers as chipotles and guajillos for your powders. Select brittle dried peppers for this purpose, or put pliant dried peppers into an oven set at 350 degrees F for 10 minutes to dry them out.

Clean all the coffee out of the grinder. Stem and seed the pepper and cut it into pieces small enough to fit easily into the grinder. Grind the pepper for a minute or so until it yields a fine powder. Remember to clean the pepper out of the grinder or you'll have some very interesting coffee the next morning.

Soaking & Pureeing Dried Chiles There's not much to it. Just put the dried chiles in a bowl with enough hot water to cover them. Put a saucer or an upside down coffee mug on top to keep the peppers submerged. Leave them there until they are soft. It usually takes from 15 or 30 minutes. Chipotles are very hard and tend to take longer. You can speed up the process by simmering them gently in water on the stove top.

If you're making stuffed peppers, be sure to take the chiles out of the water before they get too soft, or they will fall apart when you try to stuff them. Check them after 15 minutes.

If you're making a chile puree, you want the peppers very soft, so you can leave them in the water a little longer. When they are soft enough, pull the stems off and scoop out the seeds. Put the flesh in the blender with enough of the soaking water to get the blades turning. Puree until smooth. Chile peppers vary in size, so you'll have to estimate how much puree you'll get by checking the size of the peppers. Anchos yield the most puree, guajillos and other shiny-skinned peppers yield very little. When selecting peppers to make a puree, use the softest, most pliable ones available.

You can boost the flavor of the puree a little by soaking the peppers in stock instead of hot water. If you're making a sauce for chicken enchiladas, then you can use hot chicken stock. Beef stock is good for beef dishes or chili, while turkey stock is good for turkey mole.

Handling Chile Peppers It's wise to wear rubber gloves when handling jalapeños, serranos, and especially habaneros. Get a little juice from the cut-up pepper on your face or in your eyes, and you can count on 10 minutes of sheer agony. If you don't have rubber gloves, use a piece of plastic wrap to hold the pepper while you cut it. Clean the knife and the cutting board immediately with hot, soapy water. If your hands get into the pepper juice, try soaking them for a few minutes in a mild bleach solution.

CHEESES ♣ ♣ ♣

QUESO FRESCO, the most common cheese of Mexico, is a bland white cheese similar to farmer cheese or ricotta that does not melt when heated.

QUESO BLANCO is a crumbly, hard-pressed version of queso fresco that is sold in rectangular blocks and resembles an unsalty feta.

OAXACAN STRING CHEESE is a Mexican variety of mozzarella that has been stretched into rope-like strands and twisted into a ball.

CORN ♣ ♣ ♣ Select the sweetest, freshest corn on the cob you can find. For recipes that specify roasted corn: Place unshucked ears of corn in an

oven set at 350 degrees F and roast for 30 minutes, or until kernels are soft. Shuck the corn, remove the silk, cut the kernels from the cob, and proceed as directed.

EPAZOTE ໖ ໖ ໖ Prized as a pungent herb in southern Mexico, epazote is called pigweed by gardeners in the United States. Once seldom used in northern Mexican or Tex-Mex cooking, it is enjoying a new popularity because it is a traditional seasoning with black beans. Although often difficult to find in the grocery store, it is, oddly enough, easy to find in your garden. It has a jagged leaf that looks something like marijuana and has a strong soapy smell vaguely reminiscent of cilantro. If you pull some up and decide to use it in your cooking, consult an herbalist, botanist, or gardening expert to be sure you've got the right stuff. Pigweed is so common, however, that once you can identify it, you'll never have to buy it again.

GARLIC ໖ ໖ ໖ Roasting garlic gives it a sweeter, milder flavor, so we use a roasted garlic puree rather than raw garlic in most of our recipes. It is a great ingredient to have on hand for all kinds of dishes. To make roasted garlic puree: Preheat an oven to 350 degrees F. Slice off the pointy end from 3 large heads of garlic, then cut each whole head in half crosswise, exposing the cloves. Brush the half heads with 1 tablespoon olive oil and arrange the heads in a small baking dish. Add water to a depth of $1/2$ inch and cover the dish with a lid or aluminium foil. Bake for 35 to 40 minutes, or until the garlic runs like toothpaste when squeezed. Remove from the oven and, when cool enough to handle, squeeze the whole head, collecting the garlic paste in a small bowl. Cover and store the puree in the refrigerator for up to 1 week. You should have about $3/4$ cup.

HIBISCUS (JAMAICA) ໖ ໖ ໖ *Agua fresca de jamaica* is a lemonadelike drink made with the reddish purple blossom covers of the hibiscus, also called roselle and Jamaican sorrel. They look like purple flowers (they're actually calyxes). We use dried hibiscus to make a syrup for flavoring margaritas (see page 17).

HOJA SANTA ໖ ໖ ໖ The large, fuzzy, elephant ear–shaped leaves of the hoja santa plant may be used fresh or dried. The plant grows well in Texas, although a good frost will kill it back to the roots. The herb tastes a lot like anise.

MEXICAN MARIGOLD MINT ໖ ໖ ໖ Mexican marigold mint (Tagetes lucida), which grows like a weed in most parts of Texas, is a wonderfully fragrant herb that's also known as Texas tarragon. The marigold part of its name comes from the orange flowers that bloom on the mature plant. It has a strong anise flavor and must be used sparingly. In parts of Mexico, where it is called hierba de las nubes, it is used primarily for medicinal teas.

MEXICAN OREGANO ໖ ໖ ໖ Mexican oregano is a member of the verbena family and is very different from Mediterranean oregano. It can be found dried in Mexican markets and some supermarkets, but it is sometimes difficult to find fresh. Planting a little in your garden is the best guarantee of having some on hand.

MOLCAJETE ໖ ໖ ໖ The three-legged stone mortar, or *molcajete*, is the blender of ancient Mexican cooking. (The pestle is called a *tejolote*.) Although it has been replaced by the more convenient electric appliance in much of Mexico, the *molcajete* is still considered superior to the blender for making salsas, guacamole, and other blended mixtures that need to retain some of their chunkiness. And in the case of guacamole, it also serves as an attractive serving dish.

Molcajetes are easy to find in Mexican markets

and are usually pretty cheap. They must be seasoned before using, however, as the porous rock usually contains a lot of grit. First rinse as much of the grit out of the mortar as you can, then grind a couple of fresh chile peppers in it. Discard the pepper mash and put the *molcajete* in a hot oven or in the sun until it dries out. The *molcajete* always retains a little of the flavor of the last thing you ground in it.

PRICKLY PEAR CACTUS PADDLES (NOPALITOS)

The Spanish name for the prickly pear cactus is *nopal*, the plural is *nopales*. The cactus paddles are called *nopalitos*, and they are eaten as a vegetable. But before they can be sliced and cooked, they must be scraped clean of the tiny barbed spines called glochids. Cleaning cactus pads requires gloves and careful handling. A spineless variety of prickly pear is now being cultivated in Texas, and it is an excellent product. If you can't find spineless nopalitos, look for the packaged variety. Many grocery stores that cater to Mexican communities sell 10-ounce packages of precleaned, presliced nopalitos in the produce section. These are well worth the extra cost. If you decide to clean your own and get a barb stuck in your finger, take this advice from cactus expert Dr. Peter Felker of Texas A&M University: "Use a pair of tweezers! Your first inclination when you can't get hold of the little things with your fingers is to try and pull them out with your teeth. It you do that, odds are you will end up with a cactus barb stuck in your tongue. And that's a mistake you won't make twice."

PRICKLY PEAR FRUIT

Opuntia ficus-indica, better known as prickly pear, provides the most common of Mexico's cactus fruits. The fruits are called *tunas* in Mexico, and they come in a wide variety of colors. The purplish red *tuna* is the one we use in our margarita recipes. Prickly pear fruits are cultivated on plantations in Mexico, and they are much larger than the fruits of wild cactus. Like the paddles, the fruits have clusters of barbs and must be handled carefully. You will usually see a pair of tongs beside a bin of prickly pear fruits in a grocery store. Use them to select the fruits. Use rubber gloves to clean them when you get home.

RICE

Long-grain white rice will work fine in most recipes in this book, but we much prefer the new long-grain-basmati hybrid called Texmati. It is aromatic and retains a nutty firmness when cooked. Basmati is an excellent substitute.

TAMARIND

Tamarind comes from a pod that looks like a giant bean. The pulp is dark brown and sticky and has a complex tart flavor that has long been a favorite seasoning in Indian food. In Mexico it is used primarily in *agua fresca de tamarindo*, a lemonadelike drink. You can often find prepared tamarind paste for sale in Asian and Mexican groceries. To extract the pulp from whole beans, soak the beans in hot water until the peel comes away easily, then peel the beans and mash the pulp to remove the large, round seeds.

TOMATILLOS

Husk-covered tomatillos, which are tart and nearly always cooked before being eaten, are essential to Tex-Mex and Mexican cooking. They are widely available in grocery stores: look for firm, unblemished tomatillos with tight husks. Many Mexican cooks say that the smaller tomatillos are more flavorful.

TEJANO

The word *tejano* means simply "Texan" in modern Spanish, but it has taken on much wider connotations. It is sometimes used as a Spanish language synonym for Tex-Mex.

Mexican-Americans of Texan ancestry also call themselves Tejanos. Some Tejano families trace their heritage back to the state's original settlers.

They are the Texas equivalent of New England families whose ancestors came over on the Mayflower. As Tejanos are fond of pointing out, they didn't immigrate to the United States, the border moved south. Unlike Mexican nationals or recent immigrants from Mexico, Tejanos are proud to call their food Tex-Mex.

TEX-MEX ❧ ❧ ❧ *Barron's Food Lover's Companion* defines Tex-Mex as "a term given to food (as well as music, etc.) based on the combined cultures of Texas and Mexico."

TORTILLAS ❧ ❧ ❧ Many grocery stores stock a wide variety of tortillas these days. There are plain and flavored flour tortillas, fluffy white corn tortillas, and old-fashioned corn tortillas. The old-fashioned corn ones, sometimes called enchilada tortillas, are the most common. They are very thin and somewhat leathery, but hold up well in cooking. Use these for frying and save the flour tortillas and fluffy white corn tortillas for serving at the table.

Heating Tortillas Store-bought flour or corn tortillas need to be heated before serving. The easiest method is to wrap them in foil and stick them in a 350 degree F oven for 5 to 10 minutes. Corn tortillas can also be wrapped in a clean dish towel that has been slightly dampened and then put into the oven. The moisture from the towel will steam them slightly and improve their texture as they warm up.

When you only need a few flour tortillas, it's even easier to put them into an ungreased skillet over medium heat and to flip them quickly as they warm, shuffling the tortillas until each side has been in contact with the skillet for 10 seconds or so.

Frying Tortillas Don't try to fry flour tortillas or the white corn tortillas, which contain some wheat flour. It doesn't work. You need plain corn tortillas for frying, the staler the better. You may be tempted just to use prepackaged taco shells or tostadas. Resist that temptation. A freshly fried tortilla makes a world of difference in flavor and texture. Once you get the hang of it, it's really pretty easy. We prefer peanut oil for frying since it gives the tortillas a nice nutty taste, but canola or corn oil will work, too.

Keeping the oil just hot enough is the hardest part of frying tortillas. The perfect temperature is 350 degrees F. At this level the tortilla will bubble relatively gently. If the tortilla bubbles violently, it will get too crisp too fast and overbrown on the edges. Once you have the oil hot enough, turn the burner down to medium or medium-high.

Pour the oil into a small pan or skillet. How much oil you use depends on the size of the pan. The oil needs to be at least $1/2$ inch deep. Place the pan over high heat. It will take 5 to 7 minutes for the oil to reach the optimum frying temperature of 350 degrees F. If you start with a medium flame, it will take a little longer, but you won't risk burning the oil.

TO FRY A TOSTADA A tostada is just a corn tortilla fried flat. Slip the tortilla into the hot oil. When it starts to harden, turn it several times with tongs so it gets done on both sides. This should take about 1 minute. Drain on paper towels.

TO FRY TACO SHELLS Preheat an oven to warm (200 degrees F). Put several paper towels inside of a sheet-cake pan. Slip a tortilla into the hot oil. Flip it over after 5 seconds. After another 5 seconds, as the tortilla starts to harden a little, use a pair of tongs to flip one side up to form a U shape. Hold it there for 10 seconds until it sets in that position. Flip the U over and fry the side that's been elevated for 10 seconds. Spread the tongs on the inside of the U to keep the taco shell open if it starts closing up. You want the taco shell firm but flexible, so it doesn't shatter when you eat it. The whole process should take about 1 minute. If the taco shells are getting crisp too fast, turn down the heat. As you finish each taco shell, put it in the cake pan and put the pan in the oven to keep the tacos shells warm.

TO FRY CHALUPA SHELLS Cut the tortillas into approximately 4-inch rounds. (You can use a 12-ounce coffee can, or the plastic top that comes with it, as a cutting guide.) Reserve the scraps. Fry the 4-inch tortilla rounds as for tostadas.

TO FRY TORTILLA CHIPS Chips are the exception to the rule. You want chips to be as crisp as possible, so you can fry them fast in hotter oil (380 degrees F). Cut the tortillas into quarters or smaller. Fry in very hot oil for about 45 seconds, or until lightly browned, stirring constantly to prevent sticking. Drain on paper towels. Salt while warm.

Oven-Drying Tortillas If you want to cut down on the fat in your fried tortillas recipes, you can take an extra step and dry the tortillas in the oven before frying them. This is also a good idea if you're trying to fry very fresh tortillas. Dried tortillas absorb less oil but retain a good corn flavor. Preheat an oven to 300 degrees F. Spread the tortillas on the oven rack and weigh them down with an empty baking sheet to prevent them from curling. Bake for 15 to 20 minutes, or until very leathery. Then fry as usual.

Tortilla Scraps You can use leftover or stale tortillas in the recipe for chilaquiles (page 46) or to make tortilla wisps to use as a garnish (see following). You can also cut the tortilla scraps into pieces and fry them in hot oil to make tortilla chips.

Tortilla Wisps Cut whole tortillas or tortilla scraps into extremely fine strips. Fluff them into curls and fry them for a few seconds in hot oil. Remove them with a slotted spoon and drain on paper towels. Use the wisps as a garnish.

VANILLA 🍃 🍃 🍃 One of Mexico's greatest contributions to the food world is vanilla. Unfortunately, the Mexican vanilla industry has been rocked by scandals. Reportedly, much of what sells for vanilla extract in Mexico is not pure vanilla.

The best way to get all the flavor of vanilla in your food is to use the vanilla bean itself rather than the extract. Most of the whole vanilla beans sold in gourmet stores come from Madagascar and are of excellent quality. The recipes in this book specify that you split the bean lengthwise and scrape the seeds into the pot. You can drop the shells into your sugar canister to give your sugar a wonderful vanilla scent.

If the vanilla beans are dry or especially small, you might want to consider another alternative: Break the whole unsplit bean into several pieces, grind it in a clean coffee grinder, and use the whole ground vanilla bean in the recipe. The dark flecks will discolor the food slightly, but you get more vanilla flavor this way.

All of the ingredients in this book are common throughout the Southwest and most of the rest of the country. If you have a Mexican market in your town, you should have no trouble finding everything you need. If you can't find some of the fresh produce we use, the item you're looking for may just be out of season. If you live in an area where Mexican ingredients are unavailable, try these mail-order sources:

DON ALFONSO FOODS

P.O. Box 201988
Austin, TX 78720
800-456-6100
Catalog available
Achiote paste, dried Mexican oregano,
extensive selection of dried chiles.

TEXAS SPICE COMPANY

P.O. Box 3769
Austin, TX 78764
512-444-2223
Catalog available
Dried chiles and freshly ground chile
powders, achiote powder (you add your
own vinegar), ground cumin, dried
Mexican oregano.

PENDRY'S

1221 Manufacturing Street
Dallas, TX 75207
800-533-1870
Catalog $2
Molcajetes, dried chiles, cumin,
Mexican oregano.

IT'S ABOUT THYME

11726 Mancacha Road
Austin, TX 78748
512-280-1192
Plants for your garden or greenhouse,
including Mexican marigold mint, epazote,
Mexican oregano, and *hoja santa*.

MOZZARELLA COMPANY

2944 Elm Street
Dallas, TX 75226
800-798-2954
Catalog available
Handmade Mexican-style cheeses,
including Oaxacan string cheese and
queso fresco.

Bibliography

Andrews, Jean. *Peppers: The Domesticated Capsicums.* Austin: University of Texas Press, 1984.

Barrios, Virginia B. *A Guide to Tequila, Mexcal, and Pulque.* Mexico D.F.: Minutiae Mexicana, S. S., 1988.

Bayless, Rick. *Authentic Mexican.* New York: Morrow, 1987.

Beard, James. *James Beard's American Cookery.* Boston: Little Brown, 1972.

DeWitt, Dave. *The Food Lover's Handbook to the Southwest.* Rocklin, Calif.: Prima, 1992.

Hearon, Reed. *La Parilla.* San Francisco: Chronicle Books, 1996.

Herbst, Sharon Tyler. *Food Lover's Companion.* New York: Barron's, 1990.

Hutson, Lucinda. *The Herb Garden Cookbook.* Austin: Texas Monthly Press, 1987.

———. *Tequila!* Berkeley, Calif.: Ten Speed Press, 1995.

Kennedy, Diana. *The Cuisines of Mexico.* New York: Harper & Row, 1972.

Klein, Bob. *Beer Lover's Rating Guide.* New York: Workman, 1995.

Miller, Mark. *The Great Salsa Book.* Berkeley, Calif.: Ten Speed Press, 1994.

Thorne, John. "The Bean Cooking Revolution." *Simple Cooking.* March/April 1996.

———. *Serious Pig.* New York: North Point Press, 1996.

Tolbert, Frank X. *A Bowl of Red.* New York: Doubleday, 1972.

Table of Equivalents

The exact equivalents in the following tables have been rounded for convenience.

LIQUID AND DRY MEASURES

U.S.	METRIC
$^{1}/_{4}$ teaspoon	1.25 milliliters
$^{1}/_{2}$ teaspoon	2.5 milliliters
1 teaspoon	5 milliliters
1 tablespoon (3 teaspoons)	15 milliliters
1 fluid ounce (2 tablespoons)	30 milliliters
$^{1}/_{4}$ cup	60 milliliters
$^{1}/_{3}$ cup	80 milliliters
1 cup	240 milliliters
1 pint (2 cups)	480 milliliters
1 quart (4 cups, 32 ounces)	960 milliliters
1 gallon (4 quarts)	3.84 liters
1 ounce (by weight)	28 grams
$^{1}/_{4}$ pound (4 ounces)	114 grams
1 pound	454 grams
2.2 pounds	1 kilogram

LENGTH MEASURES

U.S.	METRIC
$^{1}/_{8}$ inch	3 millimeters
$^{1}/_{4}$ inch	6 millimeters
$^{1}/_{2}$ inch	12 millimeters
1 inch	2.5 centimeters

OVEN TEMPERATURES

FAHRENHEIT	CELSIUS	GAS
250	120	$^{1}/_{2}$
275	140	1
300	150	2
325	160	3
350	180	4
375	190	5
400	200	6
425	220	7
450	230	8
475	240	9
500	260	10

Index

Index

Index